At Issue

Are America's Wealthy Too Powerful?

Other Books in the At Issue Series:

At Issue

Are America's Wealthy Too Powerful?

Ronald D. Lankford, Jr., Book Editor

GREENHAVEN PRESS
A part of Gale, Cengage Learning

GALE
CENGAGE Learning™

Detroit • New York • San Francisco • New Haven, Conn • Waterville, Maine • London

GALE
CENGAGE Learning·

Christine Nasso, *Publisher*
Elizabeth Des Chenes, *Managing Editor*

© 2011 Greenhaven Press, a part of Gale, Cengage Learning.

Gale and Greenhaven Press are registered trademarks used herein under license.

For more information, contact:
Greenhaven Press
27500 Drake Rd.
Farmington Hills, MI 48331-3535
Or you can visit our Internet site at gale.cengage.com

For product information and technology assistance, contact us at

Gale Customer Support, 1-800-877-4253
For permission to use material from this text or product, submit all requests online at www.cengage.com/permissions

Further permissions questions can be emailed to permissionrequest@cengage.com

Articles in Greenhaven Press anthologies are often edited for length to meet page requirements. In addition, original titles of these works are changed to clearly present the main thesis and to explicitly indicate the author's opinion. Every effort is made to ensure that Greenhaven Press accurately reflects the original intent of the authors. Every effort has been made to trace the owners of copyrighted material.

Cover image © Images.com/Corbis.

LIBRARY OF CONGRESS CATALOGING-IN-PUBLICATION DATA

Are America's wealthy too powerful? / Ronald D. Lankford, Jr., book editor.
    p. cm. -- (At issue)
  Includes bibliographical references and index.
  ISBN 978-0-7377-5087-4 (hbk.) -- ISBN 978-0-7377-5088-1 (pbk.)
  1. Wealth--Social aspects--United States--Juvenile literature. 2. Wealth--Moral and ethical aspects--United States--Juvenile literature. 3. Power (Social sciences)--United States--Juvenile literature. 4. Rich people--United States-- Public opinion--Juvenile literature. I. Lankford, Ronald D., 1962-
  HC110.W4A74 2010
  305.5'2340973--dc22
                                                                  2010021945

Printed in the United States of America
1 2 3 4 5 6 7 14 13 12 11 10

Contents

Introduction

Throughout U.S. history, many Americans have embraced the idea that anyone can become wealthy, that anyone can live the American dream. At the same time, Americans have also embraced the democratic idea of equality, that all citizens should have access to that dream. These two ideas, however, have the potential to clash over the balance of power. How is wealth distributed in the United States? How does this distribution affect political power? Do businesses and corporations have the power to influence what people think or, through donations, to influence politicians? For many Americans who seek the American dream, these questions are potentially troublesome.

Because of the economic system of the United States, there is no limit to how much wealth an individual can accumulate. In theory, this means that anyone can accumulate wealth. In practice, it means that at any given time, some Americans have a great deal more wealth than others. According to economist Edward N. Wolff at New York University, in 2007, 1 percent of Americans controlled 42.7 percent of the nation's financial wealth; the next 19 percent of Americans controlled 50.3 percent of the nation's wealth; the remaining 80 percent of Americans controlled 7 percent of the nation's wealth. These statistics make it clear that some Americans have a great deal more wealth than others, but they reveal little about how wealth relates to the exercise of power.

Wealth, sociologist G. William Domhoff notes, "can be seen as a 'resource' that is very useful in exercising power."[1] While "exercising power" may sound like an abstract idea, all it essentially means is the ability to buy or acquire what one wishes. Greater wealth, however, also potentially allows an individual more choice and more influence. "Wealth also can be useful in shaping the general social environment to the benefit of the wealthy," writes Domhoff, "whether through hiring public relations firms or donating money for universities, museums, music halls, and art galleries."[2]

In 2009 the Center for Responsive Politics reported that 237 members, or 44 percent, of Congress were millionaires. In terms of monetary wealth, the top ten richest persons in Congress ranged between $72 million and $251 million in net worth. Many of the presidential candidates in 2008 were also millionaires. The net worth of the major candidates ranged from Barack Obama's $1.3 million to Mitt Romney's $202 million. Likewise, candidates had access to wealth through fund raising. In 2008, John McCain was able to raise $368 million in funding, while Obama's campaign raised $745 million.

While these numbers do not prove that the wealthy have more access to government, they have led many people to observe that money and wealth are important components when considering a run for political office. Likewise, because even wealthy candidates rely on large donations, such financial statistics suggest that money can "buy" political access. "The wealthiest corporations and special interest groups usually pepper politicians with overwhelming amounts of money in hope of influencing the political process," writes the Center for Responsive Politics.[3]

A great deal of wealth in America is concentrated around big businesses and corporations. The Fortune 500, for instance, is an annual list published by *Fortune* magazine of the wealthiest public corporations. At the top of the list in 2009, ExxonMobil generated $442.85 billion in revenue; Wal-Mart generated $405.6 billion. That equaled $45.2 billion in profits for ExxonMobil and $13.4 billion for Wal-Mart. Collectively, the chief executives of the top 500 companies averaged $11.4 million in salary in 2008.

The wealth controlled by businesses and corporations impacts American society in a number of ways. Because they are in business to make a profit, corporations use their wealth to influence the public through advertising and the use or ownership of media outlets (TV stations, magazines, and so on). Business wealth, some analysts argue, also allows a small number of companies excessive control over the U.S. economy.

Corporations frequently donate money to political candidates. Between 1990 and 2010, for instance, AT&T donated over $44 million to both the Republican and Democratic parties; in the same period, Goldman Sachs donated over $31 million. While these donations do not guarantee favorable outcomes of legislation, many commentators express the view that big donors do have greater access to politicians than the average American and do have some impact on the laws that are passed.

It would be misleading to suggest that the wealthy in America are interested only in profit, political influence, and abuse of power. A great deal of wealth is donated to charities, the arts, libraries, schools, and churches, enriching every member of a given community. Still, questions concerning power and wealth in America, and the potential misuse of power, remain. While most Americans have seemingly held few objections to the concept of the accumulation of wealth, attitudes toward the wealthy tend to shift during trying economic times.

Such a shift became evident during the economic recession that emerged in 2007–08. Following the collapse of major financial institutions, many Americans began to question whether Wall Street had too much power over the economy. Both the federal bailout of many investment banks and the continued distribution of bonus checks to Wall Street employees have fueled popular anger toward corporations and government. "There is no doubt," wrote Leon Hadar for the *Business Times*, "that Americans are angry, very angry, at those who brought about this mess."[4] The multifaceted positions explored in *At Issue: Are America's Wealthy Too Powerful?* reveal that attempting to understand the relationship between wealth and power in the United States remains an important issue, one that will continue to engage Americans in new ways.

Notes

1. G. William Domhoff, "Power in America," *Who Rules America?* April 2010. http://sociology.ucsc.edu.
2. G. William Domhoff, "Power in America," *Who Rules America?* April 2010. http://sociology.ucsc.edu.
3. Center for Responsive Politics, "Heavy Hitters," OpenSecrets Blog, February 23, 2010. www.opensecrets.org.
4. Leon Hadar, "Channelling Populist Anger to Wall Street," *Business Times*, January 19, 2010.

1

American Beliefs About the Wealthy Are Changing

Michael Hiltzik

Michael Hiltzik, a Pulitzer Prize–winning columnist for the Los Angeles Times, *has worked for that newspaper for more than twenty years, covering finance, politics, and science and technology. He also served as a foreign correspondent in Africa and Russia.*

In the past, most Americans believed that they could become wealthy. Today, that belief is changing. Many Americans have seen their savings disappear while Wall Street brokers continue to receive bonuses. Because of this, a number of ideas that once seemed out of date—like the progressive income tax—may come back into style. Perhaps wealthy Americans, who have so much more money than poor Americans, should be taxed at a higher rate. While some have argued that the American economy cannot prosper without the rich, many Americans are beginning to question this assumption.

The notion that the poor always will be with us has been ingrained in our culture ever since the sermons of Moses were set down by the anonymous author of Deuteronomy.

The financial crisis of the present day raises a rather different issue, however: What should we do about the rich?

That the point is even open for discussion suggests that a sea change is taking place on the American political scene. For

Michael Hiltzik, "The Belief That the Wealthy Are Worthy Is Waning," *Los Angeles Times*, March 19, 2009. Copyright © 2009 *Los Angeles Times*. Reproduced by permission.

decades, the wealthy have been held up as people to be admired, victors in the Darwinian economic struggle by virtue of their personal ingenuity and hard work.

Americans consistently supported fiscal policies that undermined middle- and working-class interests partially because they saw themselves as rich-people-in-waiting: Given time, toil and the magic of compound interest, anyone could retire a millionaire.

Fueling Public Anger

That mind-set has all but been eradicated by the damage sustained by the average worker's nest egg, combined with the spectacle of bankers and financial engineers maintaining their lifestyles with multimillion-dollar bonuses while the submerged 99% struggle for oxygen. The price of admission to the top 1% income-earning club last year [2008] was roughly $400,000. That may account for the near-total absence of public outcry over President [Barack] Obama's proposal to raise tax rates on the wealthiest Americans—except of course from the wealthiest Americans.

One factor fueling the public fury over the AIG [American International Group, Inc.] bonuses, so inescapably in the news this week [in March 2009], is the recognition that so many huge fortunes landed in the hands of the undeserving rich. Some of them added little value to the economy but merely moved money around in novel, excessively clever and ultimately destructive ways; others are corporate executives who were ridiculously overpaid whether they succeeded or failed at their jobs.

It won't be long now, moreover, before Americans again wise up to the role of dumb luck in building wealth. By my count, roughly one-quarter of the names on the *Forbes* list of the 400 richest Americans got there by inheritance (and by no means have all of them enhanced the family fortune with their own toil or brainpower). A few years ago, it was common to think of the rich as a special breed. We may soon come around to George Orwell's view that the only difference between rich and poor is income—"The average millionaire," as he put it, "is only the average dishwasher dressed in a new suit."

The price of admission to the top 1% income-earning club last year [2008] was roughly $400,000.

The Power of the Dollar

The shift in sentiment should surprise no one. As the management sage Peter Drucker once predicted, "In the next economic downturn there will be an outbreak of bitterness and contempt for the super-corporate chieftains who pay themselves millions. In every major economic downturn in U.S. history the 'villains' have been the 'heroes' during the preceding boom." Drucker was speaking in 1997, two downturns ago.

This brings us to a couple of questions certain to become more pressing as we stagger through the fiscal and economic hangover from the Roaring Oughty-Oughts: How much does our economy depend on the rich, anyway, and why shouldn't we soak them good?

A bit of history will be useful here. The original case for a progressive income tax—that is, one levied disproportionately on larger incomes—was based less on raising revenue for the state than breaking up concentrations of wealth, inherited and otherwise. The nation's Founding Fathers considered these to be undemocratic—markers of "an aristocratic society, not a free and virtuous republic," as the tax-law expert Dennis Ventry has written.

Recent events validate the Founders' instincts. The craze for financial deregulation in Washington was fomented in part by Wall Street plutocrats brandishing lavish political donations, gifts, offers of employment and other trappings of economic power. Would Wall Street have gotten so far out of control if it had had less power to wield? No one can know for sure, but it's a question worth pondering.

There's also a social value in suppressing income inequality. In a country with only a slightly less ingrained tradition of civility than the United States, the AIG affair would provoke rioting in the streets.

How much does our economy depend on the rich, anyway, and why shouldn't we soak them good?

Taxing the Wealthy

"We live in a country with tranquility and good feelings toward each other, and that's precious," says Robert Shiller, a Yale University economist and co-author of *Animal Spirits[: How Human Psychology Drives the Economy, and Why It Matters for Global Capitalism]*, a new book about the psychology of economies. In the current crisis, "there's anger and a sense of injustice taking hold, and it's not in the interest of wealthy people—you don't want people on the poor side of town to be angry with you."

By the way, maintaining the civic institutions, police forces and public infrastructure that enable great fortunes to be made and kept costs money. Wealthy taxpayers should keep that in mind the next time they're inclined to bellyache about not getting anything from government.

As a rationale for progressive taxation, the concept of regulation and redistribution eventually yielded to the quest for revenue. Taxing large incomes was justified because that's where the money is, and, secondarily, a rich person suffers less in giving up a dollar than does a poor one.

The inflection point was the [President Franklin Delano] Roosevelt administration. FDR kept talking about the justice of chipping away at "great accumulations of wealth," but he also needed the money. The overall average tax bite on the richest Americans reached its high-water mark of nearly 59% during World War II.

A New Social Experiment

After that, even though marginal rates (the amounts charged on the last dollars) remained as high as 91%, the average tax bite on the rich fell to as little as 25% in the early '60s, largely the result of their skill in exploiting loopholes. Starting with [President] Ronald Reagan, federal income tax policy came to focus mostly on finding the rate that could produce the most revenue while provoking the minimum squawking from the wealthy chickens being plucked.

Those squawks sometimes take the form of a claim that too much taxation saps the economic value of the wealthy— their capacity to invest, to create jobs, etc. It's proper to note that years of study have unearthed no consistent evidence that taxation causes the rich to alter their investing behavior much, at least not until their tax burden reaches a point vastly higher than what Obama contemplates.

Certainly the claim of the rich to play an indispensable role in the American economy will be treated with more skepticism than in the recent past.

"The real rich—the top 1%—work very hard for reasons other than money," Reuven S. Avi-Yonah, a tax historian at the University of Michigan, told me this week. The quest for prestige, political power and self-esteem, the ability to control things and people, are all factors in their behavior.

Thanks to the financial crisis, those goals are regarded with increasing hostility by the political establishment. Certainly the claim of the rich to play an indispensable role in the American economy will be treated with more skepticism than in the recent past and their ability to preserve their loopholes and other advantages in the tax code will diminish.

Will the economy suffer as a result? The experiment is about to begin.

2

Investment Bankers Are Responsible for the American Financial Crisis

Bill Buzenberg

Bill Buzenberg is the executive director of the Center for Public Integrity. He spent more than thirty-five years as a journalist and an executive at newspapers and in public radio.

Many have supported a myth in relation to the recent collapse of the Wall Street financial markets: that the investment bankers were taken by surprise. In truth, the investment bankers played a key role in the financial collapse. These banks willingly invested money in bad loans and covered these loans with unregulated insurance. Meanwhile, government officials, despite being warned, ignored the impending collapse of markets. When the financial markets did collapse, the government neither blamed Wall Street nor admitted to the lack of oversight. Instead, the federal government bailed out the investment bankers, revealing perhaps the political connection between government and big business.

There is something of a myth surrounding the current economic crisis, how it unfolded, and the precise role of the world's largest financial institutions in the global meltdown. That myth suggests these banks and investment houses were

Bill Buzenberg, "Commentary: The Mega-Banks Behind the Meltdown," The Center for Public Integrity, May 6, 2009.

somehow surprised "victims" of unscrupulous subprime mortgage lenders, and that they could not have anticipated the damaging toxic assets that have so infected their balance sheets.

What's missing from this story is the fact that this was a self-inflicted wound for which the rest of us are picking up a massive tab. The largest American and European banks and investment houses were not the unwitting "victims" of an unforeseen financial collapse as they have so often been portrayed. The mega-banks not only invested in subprime lending institution—they were the enablers, bankrollers, and instigators driving high-interest lending, and they did so because it was so lucrative and unregulated.

Worse, in many instances these are the same financial institutions the government is now bailing out with tax revenues. How these bottomed-out banks helped cause the financial meltdown can be clearly seen in a new study by the Center for Public Integrity. The Center ran a computer analysis of every high-interest loan reported by the industry to the U.S. government from 2005 through 2007, a period that marks the peak and collapse of the subprime market. From this pool of 7.2 million loans, our investigators identified the top subprime lenders. The "Subprime 25" were responsible for nearly a trillion dollars of subprime lending, or 72 percent of all reported high-interest loans.

The "Subprime 25," which are mostly no longer in business, were largely non-bank retail lenders that needed outside financing to make their subprime loans. So where did that financing come from? The Center's study found that at least 21 of these Subprime 25 lenders were either owned outright by the biggest banks or former investment houses, or had their subprime lending hugely financed by those banks, either directly or through lines of credit. In other words, the largest American and European banks made the bubble in subprime lending possible by financing it on the front end, so they could reap the huge rewards from securitizing and selling mortgage-backed securities on the back end. The demand was insatiable, and the backing excessive. Between 2000 and 2007, underwriters of subprime mortgage-backed securities—primarily Wall Street and European investment banks—poured $2.1 trillion into the business, according to data from trade publication *Inside Mortgage Finance.*

Did these major financial institutions not understand what kind of lending was taking place? The poor quality of these loans was no secret. Many of these subprime lenders, the Center found, were forced to pay billions of dollars to settle government charges of abusive or predatory lending practices. This was a period of some of the worst mortgage lending in American history, in which regulators were nowhere to be seen, and normal income documentation and loan standards were thrown out the window. In many cases, though, the big banks really didn't care if the loans were bad. That's because they'd bought "insurance" against them—those infamous "credit default swaps." The swaps sounded good, except they were unregulated, and those selling them—like American International Group, Inc.—didn't have to maintain reserves to guard against unforeseen losses.

It was all a house of cards, and some tried to sound the alarm. A look at the historical record shows that Washington was warned repeatedly over the last decade—by consumer advocates and a handful of regulators and lawmakers—that these high-cost loans represented a systemic risk to the economy. It is hard to believe the major banks were unaware of what was going on, or what the consequences might ultimately be.

A typical warning came from William Brennan, an attorney with the Atlanta Legal Aid Society. Brennan had watched as subprime lenders earned enormous profits making mortgages to people who clearly couldn't afford them. The loans were bad for borrowers—Brennan knew that. He also knew the loans were bad for the Wall Street investors who invested in these loans, and then bought the shaky mortgages by the millions. "I think this house of cards may tumble some day, and it will mean great losses for the investors who own stock in those companies," Brennan told a Senate committee. That was in 1998. Many other unheeded warnings followed.

The truth is these mega-banks invested trillions, made billions, and took risks with their eyes wide open.

Despite such warnings, Congress, the White House, and the Federal Reserve all dithered while the subprime disaster spread. Long forgotten congressional hearings and oversight reports, as well as interviews with former officials, reveal a troubling history of missed opportunities, thwarted regulations, and abject lack of oversight. Instead, the financial industry supported more deregulation, along with an extraordinary disregard for the damage being done. This was accompanied by millions of dollars in political contributions to leading lawmakers of both parties from the same financial industry that is in such trouble today.

The truth is these mega-banks invested trillions, made billions, and took risks with their eyes wide open. Now, because they are deemed "too big to fail," they need trillions in government bailouts and guarantees to solve problems they helped create. But let's look at it another way: perhaps these mega-banks are simply "too politically connected to fail." Their unbridled political contributions and massive lobbying created the lack of regulation and oversight that led to this crisis. Where is the accountability—of management and boards, of auditors and regulators—for what has happened? It is time to set aside the myth of the mega-bank as victim.

3

Investment Bankers Are Not Responsible for the American Financial Crisis

Jim Reynolds Jr.

Jim Reynolds Jr. is the chairman and chief executive officer of Loop Capital Markets, a minority-owned investment banking firm.

Following the financial collapse of Wall Street, many commentators were quick to blame investment bankers. A number of investment bankers, however, have a history of acting responsibly. In the end, many people—not just investment bankers—were responsible for the speculation that eventually led to financial collapse. Government regulators, for instance, ignored the impending crisis. Likewise, the boards of many companies failed in their oversight duties. It is easy to blame investment bankers, but when one looks at the broader picture, it is clear that the causes of the collapse are complex and those deserving blame are numerous.

Being an investment banker has become a lonely occupation. The newspapers run articles about how you blew up the financial system of the largest nation in the free world. Commentators on business television are quick to decry the avarice that led you to do it. The administration has a person whose responsibility it is to limit the compensation of you and all your colleagues, regardless of what you do, if you work for a financial institution that has received federal monies. While the investment banker is the clear loser at the moment in today's fiscal crisis 'blame game,' will laying the blame at the foot of investment bankers hold up to scrutiny?

Loop Capital has been in business since 1997. We have never traded a collateralized debt obligation (CDO), originated a subprime mortgage, or sold a credit default swap. Perhaps more importantly, Loop has never received a dime of federal bailout money of any kind. You can imagine my bewilderment at the scorn being heaped upon investment bankers so indiscriminately when Loop Capital, and undoubtedly many other financial services firms, has nothing to do with creating the fiscal crisis, and, as a Troubled Asset Relief Program [TARP] institution selected by the Federal Reserve [System, the central banking system of the United States], everything to do with helping to fix it.

The Financial Crisis

Let's stop for a second and ask, who started this mess? The fiscal crisis was born in Washington, D.C., in the administrations of President Bill Clinton and President George W. Bush, both of whom pressured Fannie Mae and Freddie Mac [U.S. government-sponsored mortgage lenders] to accept more subprime mortgages in order to boost homeownership beyond the 65-percent level that it had been stuck at for decades. With the government fully supportive of this new, untested, subprime mortgage product, the environment was ripe for aggressive lending institutions to market subprime mortgage loans to people who wanted the American dream of homeownership, but in truth, really could not afford it.

The mortgage industry had 'evolved' to an originate-to-distribute model. In other words, take your profit and sell the loan out, or 'pass the trash.' It does not take a genius to realize that a business that, at its origin, involves no incentive to maintain lending standards will generate massive problems as the toxic mortgages wind their way through the financial system.

What is really the purpose of a 'no doc' [no documentation] loan except to ensure that you don't have in writing proof that mortgage applicants can't afford the mortgage?

Firms were ready and willing to scarf up these dubious mortgages, form CDOs with them, have them rated by the principal nationally recognized statistical rating organizations, and sell them to sophisticated investors who bought them based solely on the AAA 'Good Housekeeping seal of approval' of Moody's [Investors Service] and Standard & Poor's. The investment bankers may have put these time bombs together, but salespeople sold them, traders traded them, risk managers assessed their apparent lack of risk, and rating agency analysts approved them as AAA-rated based upon their proprietary models. When things were going well there were a lot of different firms, different occupations, standing in line to take their cut of the action.

So, if it wasn't the investment bankers, to whom do we assign blame?

The Role of Federal Regulators

Well, the mortgage origination market is a regulated market by both states and federal agencies including the Securities and Exchange Commission and the Federal Reserve System [Fed]. The bulk of these actors who provided regulatory oversight were asleep at the switch. The Fed under Alan Greenspan had never put much stock in regulating market activity, and the new market for subprime loans was considered a good thing since it had given access to housing to people who previously did not have a chance to have it. It was, in Greenspan's view, an innovation! States, which scrutinize the insurance companies and other financial service firms operating within their jurisdiction, had little interest in the aggressive sales practices of subprime lenders even after evidence of predatory lending began to surface.

The publicly traded Wall Street firms involved the creation; sales and trading of the securities that used the subprime mortgages as an input were all governed by boards of directors. Where were they? Every board has to form an audit committee. Where was the audit committee of Lehman Brothers when a firm that had its roots in the 19th century filed for bankruptcy? In a system that is founded upon the premise of strong corporate governance, the boards of these firms, the investor firms, the rating agencies, and on and on were AWOL [absent without leave, or failing to provide oversight], leaving the financial system at risk.

The rating agencies somehow managed to model the CDOs so completely incorrectly that securities previously deemed AAA-gilt-edged-rated went into default. How is this possible? The only explanation can be that the incentives of the marketing and sales staffs of these rating agencies so overwhelmed the ratings process that the firms were blinded by the profit opportunity.

The financial crisis that we are in the middle of is too critical, too costly, to seek refuge in simple-minded scapegoating and blamesmanship.

Get Rich Quick

Last, and perhaps most important, the nation's consumers, homeowners, lenders, investors, regulators and directors were so intoxicated by the 'get rich quick' opportunism provided by the burgeoning mortgage security markets that all reason and responsibility was abandoned in favor of short-term incentives. Not only was there no one to pull the punch away before the party got interesting (to channel a former Fed chairman), but there was no one to stop the indiscriminate pouring of wood alcohol into the mix while no parental authority was in sight.

The financial crisis that we are in the middle of is too critical, too costly, to seek refuge in simple-minded scapegoating and blamesmanship.

Because there are going to be many changes to our financial system, it is important that the blame be deposited at the right doorstep lest Congress and the administration devise the wrong solution to the wrong problem.

4

Rich White Men—Not Minorities—Caused the American Financial Crisis

Alex Blaze

Alex Blaze is the managing editor of the Bilerico Project, a group blog featuring the writings of lesbian, gay, bisexual, transgender, and queer (LGBTQ) activists and writers.

Many conservatives have attempted to blame the financial collapse of Wall Street in 2008 on every group except for rich, white males. In magazines like the National Review, *commentators have blamed illegal immigrants including Hispanics for diluting the housing market. Other commentators have singled out banking policies that served minority communities. Ironically, these same commentators argue that the American public should trust the rich, white men who created the crisis by bailing them out with billions of taxpayer dollars. While these arguments are often subtle, the expressed views of these commentators are nonetheless racist.*

This shouldn't be entirely unexpected, since every time there's a major problem conservatives find some way to blame it on a certain ethnic, racial, or religious group. Now they're looking for any minority to blame for what's really the absolute failure of their economic policy.

The very last thing they want the American people to see right now is that a bunch of rich, mostly white people got together and worked the system so cynically and for so long that now they're asking for a $700 billion handout to put the cherry on top of their epoch-making hustle. So they'll search for someone else to blame and hope it sticks.

A few examples of conservative talking heads blaming the crisis on minorities are after the jump. They're hoping the general equation many Americans operate under, "White = Safe," will prevent closer examination of the problem. Because it's just such a complicated financial skigamadoo, some people might actually fall for Michelle Malkin, Neil Cavuto, and the *National Review* saying that it's all really just the fault of dangerous minorities.

Every time there's a major problem conservatives find some way to blame it on a certain ethnic, racial, or religious group.

Blaming Hispanics

Here's Michelle Malkin, blaming it on Hispanics because they just didn't pay their mortgages:

> The Mother of All Bailouts has many fathers. As panicked politicians prepare to fork over $1 trillion in taxpayer funding to rescue the financial industry, they've fingered regulation, deregulation, Fannie Mae and Freddie Mac [government-sponsored mortgage lenders], the Community Reinvestment Act, [former presidents] Jimmy Carter, Bill Clinton, both Bushes [George H.W. Bush and George W. Bush], greedy banks, greedy borrowers, greedy short-sellers, and minority home ownership mau-mauers (can't call 'em greedy, that would be racist) for blame.

> But there's one giant paternal elephant in the room that has slipped notice: how illegal immigration, crime-enabling banks, and open-borders [George W.] Bush policies fueled the mortgage crisis.

It's no coincidence that most of the areas hardest hit by the foreclosure wave—Loudoun County, Va., California's Inland Empire, Stockton and San Joaquin Valley, and Las Vegas and Phoenix, for starters—also happen to be some of the nation's largest illegal-alien sanctuaries. Half of the mortgages to Hispanics are subprime (the accursed species of loan to borrowers with the shadiest credit histories). A quarter of all those subprime loans are in default and foreclosure.

Yes, the problem is all those goddamn illegals crossing the border and building McMansions in the exurbs.

The whole article is a piece of work. Like a complete racist, she doesn't know the difference between undocumented immigrants, Mexican Americans, and Hispanics. She slips between them, because *of course* every Hispanic in America is undocumented and comes from Mexico.

Mark Krikorian, over at the *National Review*, takes another tack in blaming Hispanics: Washington Mutual [Bank (WaMu)] went under because it hired too many. Here's Glenn Greenwald commenting:

National Review's Mark Krikorian notes that (1) Washington Mutual became the largest bank to fail in American history yesterday and (2) its last press release touted the fact that it was named one of America's most diverse employers, having been "honored specifically for its efforts to recruit Hispanic employees, reach out to Hispanic consumers and support Hispanic communities and organizations"; for being "named [one of] the top 60 companies for Hispanics"; for "attaining equal rights for GLBT [gay, bisexual, lesbian, transgender] employees and consumers"; for having "earned points for competitive diversity policies and programs, including the recently established Latino, African American and GLBT employee network groups"; and for being "named one of 25 Noteworthy Companies by *DiversityInc* magazine and one of the Top 50 Corporations for Supplier Diversity by *Hispanic Enterprise* magazine."

While juxtaposing these two facts—(1) WaMu has a racially and ethnically diverse workforce and (2) WaMu collapsed yesterday—the *National Review* writer headlined his post: "Cause and Effect?" He apparently believes that the reason Washington Mutual failed may be because it employed and was too accommodating to large numbers of Hispanics, African Americans and gays. . . .

Conservatives are rallying around blaming two firms [mortgage lenders Fannie Mae and Freddie Mac] that served minority clients.

Minority Clients

Rupert Murdoch's *Wall Street Journal* took a similar position, except it went on, at-length, blaming Congress's penchant for "affordable housing." It's a bit more abstract, but the op-ed is definitely borrowing the language of white resentment that surrounds affirmative action programs:

If they were not making mortgages cheaper and were creating risks for the taxpayers and the economy, what value were they providing? The answer was their affordable-housing mission. So it was that, beginning in 2004, their portfolios of subprime and Alt-A loans [alternative documentation loans] and securities began to grow. Subprime and Alt-A originations in the U.S. rose from less than 8% of all mortgages in 2003 to over 20% in 2006. During this period the quality of subprime loans also declined, going from fixed rate, long-term amortizing loans to loans with low down payments and low (but adjustable) initial rates, indicating that originators were scraping the bottom of the barrel to find product for buyers like the GSEs [government-supported enterprises].

The strategy of presenting themselves to Congress as the champions of affordable housing appears to have worked. Fannie [Mae] and Freddie [Mac] retained the support of many in Congress, particularly Democrats, and they were allowed to continue unrestrained. Rep. Barney Frank (D., Mass), for example, now the chair of the House Financial Services Committee, openly described the "arrangement" with the GSEs at a committee hearing on GSE reform in 2003: "Fannie Mae and Freddie Mac have played a very useful role in helping to make housing more affordable . . . a mission that this Congress has given them in return for some of the arrangements which are of some benefit to them to focus on affordable housing." The hint to Fannie and Freddie was obvious: Concentrate on affordable housing and, despite your problems, your congressional support is secure.

Rick Perlstein identifies the notion of blaming Freddie Mac and Fannie Mae for this crisis as racist. It makes sense, considering that even if they didn't exist, we'd still be in this mess. But conservatives are rallying around blaming two firms that served minority clients.

Welfare for the Wealthy

Then again, in an even more abstract sense, the way the solution to this crisis is being posited is racist and classist in and of itself. After years of denying basic funding to programs that help out lower-income folks, saying again and again that they were too expensive and that the people receiving them couldn't be trusted, [Treasury Secretary] Henry Paulson is asking for $700 billion to effectively give to a small group of people who are rich and mostly white and have proven themselves to be *completely irresponsible* with money.

And what's the reaction from the same people who can't be bothered to enact a food stamps program for fear that that money will get "wasted" on lobster (imagery of fictional welfare queens comes to mind)? [As Evan Newmark writes in 2008 in the *Wall Street Journal* blog Deal Journal:]

It may not seem this way, but Americans are a lucky people.

Last week, we did our best to destroy the financial system but somehow came through it. This week, Congress will have only 72 hours to ruin the Treasury's $700 billion mortgage plan before it recesses.

If our luck holds, Hank [Henry] Paulson will get the extraordinary authority he seeks. If we are really lucky, Paulson may actually fix the mess we have made. So why not give him whatever he needs?

Of course, it is easy to be outraged by the Treasury's bailout proposal. Lots of money. Lots of power. Naked, ugly dictatorial power.

"Decisions by the Treasury pursuant to the Authority of this Act are non-reviewable and committed to agency discretion, and may not be reviewed by any court of law or any administrative agency." Such language could have been drafted by any third world caudillo [military dictator].

But it wasn't. It was drafted by U.S. Treasury lawyers at the behest of the Secretary of the Treasury.

And Paulson isn't any Secretary of the Treasury. He doesn't need power. And he certainly doesn't need money.

Of course, he isn't a saint or Superman. He is awkward and an awful public speaker. But he is the one man that can serve as an honest broker between the banks and the taxpayers—between Wall Street and Washington.

He can do the right thing for the country. How many other people on Wall Street or Washington can we say that about?

Well, we could say it about all of them, again and again, if we wanted to.

That's the right-wing response to someone who's proven that he doesn't understand the current financial crisis asking for money to just hand out to a bunch of rich, mostly white men who've proven that they can't handle [it].

Compare the fact that the bailout is supposed to be instituted with no judicial or congressional review with this story from a few days ago [on September 19, 2008, in the *Detroit Free Press*] (keep in mind that food stamp spending projected for 2008 is about 5% that of the proposed bailout):

> The Michigan attorney general's office has announced 22 arrests in connection with an investigation of food stamp trafficking in Detroit.
>
> The raid of nine gas stations and convenience stores resulted in the recovery of more than $100,000.
>
> Attorney General Mike Cox announced the arrests today. He says the yearlong probe uncovered that food stamp benefits were being exchanged for cash.
>
> State and federal authorities worked on the investigation. Both storeowners and employees face charges ranging from racketeering to conspiracy. Some face up to 20 years in prison if they're convicted.

I wonder how many businesses will be raided to prevent any fraud when it comes to the bailout.

Business as Usual

It's insane how the business class, after building decades of distrust towards those who receive relatively minuscule amounts of money from social programming, is asking us to simply trust Paulson and these bankers. The difference isn't just class privilege, but white privilege, considering how imagery surrounding welfare reform constantly drifted off into racial territory.

According to Republican strategist Lee Atwater, the right-wing point of view on social spending actually started on racial lines:

> You start out in 1954 by saying, "N-----, n-----, n-----." By 1968 you can't say "n-----"—that hurts you. Backfires. So

you say stuff like forced busing, states' rights and all that stuff. You're getting so abstract now [that] you're talking about cutting taxes, and all these things you're talking about are totally economic things and a by-product of them is [that] blacks get hurt worse than whites.

And subconsciously maybe that is part of it. I'm not saying that. But I'm saying that if it is getting that abstract, and that coded, that we are doing away with the racial problem one way or the other. You follow me—because obviously sitting around saying, "We want to cut this," is much more abstract than even the busing thing, and a hell of a lot more abstract than "N-----, n-----."

If a bank gives out a loan to someone they know *won't be able to pay back . . . it's the bank's fault.*

All that white privilege that Wall Street bankers are trading in right now makes the fact that conservatives are looking for some way to pin this all on minorities even more sick.

Besides that, pinning the blame on borrowers is just another distraction. Sorry, if a bank gives out a loan to someone they *know* won't be able to pay back because they *know* they'll get a profit by selling that loan in a bond and then selling credit default swaps on it, it's the bank's fault. They said they shouldn't be regulated because they could handle it themselves, so this is either their own problem to fix or we admit that they can't be left with so little regulation and that they're too important to the economy to be left to their own devices.

But that doesn't help the wealthy people who profited from this mess, so they search for a scapegoat. I don't know if we're going to go down that path in America. Considering what happened when other economic crises in history got blamed on a minority, it's not going to be pretty if we do.

5

Loans to Minorities Fueled the American Financial Crisis

Michelle Malkin

Michelle Malkin is a conservative columnist and a contributor to the Fox News Channel. She is the author of several books, including Unhinged: Exposing Liberals Gone Wild *and* Culture of Corruption: Obama and His Team of Tax Cheats, Crooks, and Cronies.

Politicians have pointed to numerous factors that led to the recent financial crisis, but they are reluctant to point to such causes as fraudulent home loans made to minorities. Many of the areas in the United States experiencing the highest foreclosure rates are also home to some of the largest numbers of illegal aliens. For many years, banks have engaged in fraudulent lending practices, granting loans to Hispanics and other minorities with insufficient documentation. These practices led to the need for massive government bailouts, funded by responsible American taxpayers.

The Mother of All Bailouts has many fathers. As panicked politicians prepare to fork over $1 trillion in taxpayer funding to rescue the financial industry, they've fingered regulation, deregulation, Fannie Mae and Freddie Mac [government-sponsored mortgage lenders], the Community Reinvestment Act, [former presidents] Jimmy Carter, Bill Clinton, both Bushes [George H.W. Bush and George W. Bush],

Michelle Malkin, "Illegal Loans: A Criminal Business," *National Review Online*, September 24, 2008. Copyright © 2008 by National Review, Inc., 215 Lexington Avenue, New York, NY 10016. Reproduced by permission.

greedy banks, greedy borrowers, greedy short-sellers, and minority home ownership mau-mauers (can't call 'em greedy, that would be racist) for blame.

But there's one giant paternal elephant in the room that has slipped notice: how illegal immigration, crime-enabling banks, and open-borders [George W.] Bush policies fueled the mortgage crisis.

It's no coincidence that most of the areas hardest hit by the foreclosure wave—Loudoun County, Va., California's Inland Empire, Stockton and San Joaquin Valley, and Las Vegas and Phoenix, for starters—also happen to be some of the nation's largest illegal-alien sanctuaries. Half of the mortgages to Hispanics are subprime (the accursed species of loan to borrowers with the shadiest credit histories). A quarter of all those subprime loans are in default and foreclosure.

Regional reports across the country have decried the subprime meltdown's impact on illegal-immigrant "victims." A July [2008] report showed that in seven of the ten metro areas with the highest foreclosure rates, Hispanics represented at least one-third of the population; in two of those areas— Merced and Salinas [and] Monterey, Calif.—Hispanics comprised half the population. The amnesty-promoting National Council of La Raza and its development fund have received millions in federal funds to "counsel" their constituents on obtaining mortgages with little to no money down; the group almost succeeded in attaching a $10-million earmark for itself in one of the housing bills passed this spring.

Illegal immigration, crime-enabling banks, and open-borders [George W.] Bush policies fueled the mortgage crisis.

Fraudulent Loans to Illegal Aliens

For the last five years, I've reported on the rapidly expanding illegal-alien home-loan racket. The top banks clamoring for their handouts as their profits plummet, led by Wachovia and Bank of America, launched aggressive campaigns to woo illegal-alien homebuyers. The quasi-governmental Wisconsin Housing and Economic Development Authority jumped in to guarantee home loans to illegal immigrants. The *Washington Post* noted, almost as an afterthought in a 2005 report: "Hispanics, the nation's fastest-growing major ethnic or racial group, have been courted aggressively by real estate agents, mortgage brokers, and programs for first-time buyers that offer help with closing costs. Ads proclaim: '*Sin verificacion de ingresos! Sin verificacion de documento!*'—which loosely translates as, 'Income tax forms are not required, nor are immigration papers.'"

In addition, fraudsters have engaged in massive house-flipping rings using illegal aliens as straw buyers. Among many examples cited by the FBI: a conspiracy in Las Vegas involving a former Nevada First Residential Mortgage [Services Corporation] branch manager who directed loan officers and processors in the origination of 233 fraudulent Federal Housing Administration loans valued at over $25 million. The defrauders manufactured and submitted false employment and income documentation for borrowers; most were illegal immigrants from Mexico. To date, the FBI reported, "Fifty-eight loans with a total value of $6.2 million have gone into default, with a loss to the Housing and Urban Development Department of over $1.9 million."

It's the tip of the iceberg. Thanks to lax Bush administration–approved policies allowing illegal aliens to use "matricula consular cards" and taxpayer identification numbers to open bank accounts, more forms of mortgage fraud have burgeoned. Moneylenders still have no access to a verification system to check Social Security numbers before approving loans.

In an interview about rampant illegal-alien home-loan fraud, a spokeswoman for the U.S. General Accounting Office [currently the Government Accountability Office] told me five years ago: "[C]onsidering the size of Los Angeles, New York, Chicago, Houston, and other large cities throughout the United States known to be inundated with illegal aliens, I don't think the federal government is willing to expose this problem for financial reasons as well as for fear of political repercussions."

The chickens are coming home to roost. And law-abiding, responsible taxpayers are going to pay for it.

6

Wall Street Financiers Manipulate the Stock Market to Benefit Themselves

David C. Korten

David C. Korten, the cofounder and board chair of Yes! *magazine, is the author of* When Corporations Rule the World.

In recent years, Wall Street has created an economic system that only serves the needs of the wealthy. Unlike Main Street—local businesses and working people—Wall Street did not create jobs or wealth for investment. Wall Street's speculation became even more reckless because of the lack of government oversight. When the financial system collapsed in 2008, citizens' tax dollars were needed to bail out Wall Street. Because of Wall Street's irresponsibility, it is time to revive measures that regulate the financial markets. Bank and financial institutions should support Main Street, instead of Wall Street.

Events of the past few weeks have exposed the danger of a financial system devoted to reckless speculation that produces nothing of real value and, as we are now being told, presents a risk to the whole global economy. The Bush administration proposes handing $700 billion to Treasury Secretary Paulson to disburse—without oversight or review—to those who created the current mess. Spending what many analysts believe will grow to at least a trillion dollars to prop up this predatory system for a few more months, or even years, seems less than a great idea, which hopefully makes this a teachable moment.

David C. Korten, "Main Street Before Wall Street," *Yes! Magazine*, September 24, 2008. Reproduced by permission.

We might start with the lesson that there is an essential role for government. Market fundamentalists have long argued that markets freed from governmental interference self-correct. We can now see clearly that the more Wall Street freed itself from regulatory oversight, the more its most powerful players manipulated markets and politics to their personal benefit. The more reckless their risk taking became, the greater the instability of the financial system, and the greater the threat to the rest of the economy.

So what would a healthy financial system look like? Let's start with the relationship between Main Street and Wall Street. Main Street is the world of local businesses and working people engaged in producing and exchanging real goods and services—a world of real wealth. Wall Street as it now exists is a world of pure money in which the sole game is to use money to make money for people who have money—a world of speculative gains and unearned claims against the real wealth of Main Street.

Money, an essential medium of exchange, makes modern economic life possible. In our current money system, the money that Main Street depends on to facilitate productive economic exchange and investment is created when Wall Street's private banks issue loans. You might say that the business of Wall Street is creating money. This does not in itself create wealth. Money is only an accounting chit useful as a medium of exchange. Wealth creation is the business of Main Street. This suggests that the only legitimate reason for the existence of Wall Street is to provide an orderly flow of money to meet the needs of Main Street.

Wall Street performed its appropriate tasks reasonably well so long as public regulatory authorities put in place subsequent to the financial crash of 1929 held it accountable to Main Street interests. As it liberated itself from public oversight, however, Wall Street turned from serving Main Street to preying on it to generate outsized financial rewards for its biggest players. It created a mind-boggling variety of "heads I win, tails you lose" financial games.

It used deceptive practices to encourage people to run up credit card and mortgage debts far beyond their means to repay, and then hit the victims with special fees and usurious interest rates as they inevitably fell behind in their payments. To get the high-risk mortgages off their balance sheets, the banks sold them to brokers who packaged them into tradable securities with inflated quality ratings. The banks that made the decision to extend the bad credit collected their fees and passed the risk on to others. Proceeds from the sale of the overrated securities were used to finance more lending to unqualified borrowers. Many of these overrated securities ultimately ended up in the portfolios of retirement funds, passing the risk back to Main Street workers and pensioners who had no voice in any of the decisions involved.

Wall Street also found it profitable to merge regulated banks with unregulated investment houses to facilitate insider dealing and finance a proliferation of highly leveraged hedge funds and private equity funds that specialize in gambling with other people's money using exotic financial instruments no one fully understands.

In 2007, the fifty highest paid private investment fund managers averaged $588 million in compensation— 19,000 times as much as average worker pay.

The players and their apologists claimed they were creating wealth, providing market liquidity, increasing economic efficiency, and stabilizing markets. In fact, they created and profited from financial and real estate bubbles and debt pyramids that used borrowed money to create paper assets that became collateral for more borrowing to create more paper assets to justify compensation packages for themselves in the hundreds of millions of dollars. It may be legal, but it is not wealth creation. It is an act of theft made possible by abuse of the legally sanctioned power of a private banking system to create money out of nothing and direct it to use by financial predators engaged in expropriating the real wealth of Main Street for exorbitant fees.

In 2007, the fifty highest paid private investment fund managers, averaged $588 millions in compensation—19,000 times as much as average worker pay. They said they were worth it because they were so smart and productive. Now that their bets don't look so good, they think Main Street taxpayers should pony up to cover the losses of the firms they created to generate these handsome management fees.

Rather than seeking to restore the health of Wall Street's predatory private institutions, a proper plan would seek to rid Wall Street of its purely predatory elements while dismantling and reassembling its useable institutions to create a new system accountable to the needs of Main Street. Here are some of the basics.

Hedge funds and private equity funds pose great risks to society while performing no beneficial function. They should be dismantled.

It is time to revive antitrust to break up all excessive concentrations of corporate power.

As Senator Bernie Sanders has recently said, "If a company is too big to fail, it is too big to exist." Adam Smith, revered by many as the founding prophet of capitalism, cautioned against any concentration of economic power that might be used to avoid market discipline, manipulate market prices, and extract unearned profits. He had a very good idea. It's an important market principle.

It is time to revive antitrust to break up all excessive concentrations of corporate power and particularly the banking conglomerates that have been fueling speculation in global financial markets. To meet the financial needs of Main Street, create a system of federally regulated, community banks that fulfill the classic textbook function of acting as intermediaries between local people looking for a secure place for their savings and local people who need a loan to buy a home or finance a business.

Proceeds from taxes on the ill-gotten gains of those who created the financial mess can be used to make whole the pensioners, home owners, and credit card holders the system victimized.

Only a thoroughgoing redesign of Wall Street offers prospect of a real solution.

I grew up believing that a strong middle class is a foundation of democracy and the American ideal. This would be a great time to get serious about a broader legislative agenda to restore the middle class by restoring a progressive tax system, raising the minimum wage, and assuring every American has access to the basics of a decent life. And while we are creating a tax code to favor Main Street over Wall Street we should include provisions to discourage absentee ownership and speculation by making them unprofitable.

Perhaps the most important of all the needed reform measures is to make money creation a public function and strip private banks of their ability to create money out of nothing by issuing loans at interest against unsecured demand deposits.

These are not small steps. Their implementation would likely cause significant temporary disruption, but no more than the disruption that inevitably lies ahead if the current system of predatory finance remains in place. Use the trillion dollars to help the people who are creating real wealth and let the fat-cat speculators take their lumps. Only a thoroughgoing redesign of Wall Street offers prospect of a real solution. Anything else is only a costly temporal, Band-Aid.

7

Wall Street Bailout Recipients Should Not Pay Bonuses to Employees

Ruth Conniff

Ruth Conniff covers national politics for the Progressive *and is a voice of the* Progressive *on many TV and radio programs.*

The federal government decided to bail out American International Group, Inc. (AIG) to avoid the disruption of international markets that would result from allowing AIG to go through bankruptcy. At the time of writing, the federal government had given $173 billion to AIG, and AIG had spent $165 million to pay bonuses to its top executives. Members of the Senate and even President Barack Obama demanded that the bonuses be returned. Although AIG chief executive officer Edward Liddy explained that the bonuses were a contractual obligation and necessary to retain top talent, these arguments did not prove convincing in light of the fact that the contracts would have been voided in bankruptcy (which is where AIG was headed before the bailout) and that many of the top executives left the company with their bonuses in hand.

Democrats from Andrew Cuomo to Barney Frank to Barack Obama are demanding that the 418 AIG [American International Group, Inc.] employees who received bonuses give them back. Sure, it's outrageous that the very people who drove AIG off the cliff, along with a whole lot of other fi-

Ruth Conniff, "Forget AIG Bonuses—The Next Bailout Is Here," *The Progressive*, March 18, 2009. Copyright © 2009 The Progressive, Inc. Reproduced by permission of the *The Progressive*, 409 East Main Street, Madison, WI 53703. www.progressive.org.

nancial firms, walked away with million-dollar bonuses paid with taxpayer bailout money. But as the *Wall Street Journal* opinion page points out, "Taxpayers have already put up $173 billion, or more than a thousand times the amount of those bonuses, to fund the government's AIG 'rescue.'"

And there is more to come.

The Obama administration is putting the finishing touches on another big bank bailout. Called the Public-Private Investor Partnership (PPIP), it is the brainchild of the Treasury Secretary from Wall Street, Tim Geithner. Under the plan, the government will give our money to hedge fund managers to buy "toxic" assets for more than they are worth. The banks that created these toxic turkeys will use the money from the sales to recapitalize themselves. Everyone comes out ahead except, of course, the taxpayers, who are essentially funneling money to hedge funds to buy bad assets for more than they are worth. The other bonus for the banks in this plan, as Yves Smith points out, is that they get to avoid giving the toxic assets any real market value. Less transparency and more transfers of wealth from taxpayers to hedge fund managers.

So much for the "free market."

Yves Smith writes: "This is what readers ought to be upset about. The AIG bonuses are rounding error, and a done deal. This (the PPIP) is billions to avoid price discovery . . ."

$750 billion, to be precise—plus what remains of the $700 billion bank bailout Congress already approved.

Smith reports that the bailout will likely have two parts: a subsidy to the hedge funds that buy the bad assets, and another one for the banks that sell them, to make up for the low prices investors are willing to pay. It's socialism for bankers and hedge fund managers.

Meanwhile, as AIG CEO Edward Liddy testified on Capitol Hill Wednesday, members of Congress were up in arms about the bonuses he says he was "contractually obligated" to pay executives. Liddy once claimed he had to pay the money in order to retain the talented financial products executives who helped run the company into the ground. The fact that 52 of them left AIG, cash in hand, dampened that argument. On the Hill today, Liddy called on AIG employees to "do the right thing" and return "at least half" of the money if they got a bonus of more than $100,000. I guess a $50,000 bonus is what passes for punishment on Wall Street for putting your company into bankruptcy—or what would have been bankruptcy had the government not bailed out AIG.

And speaking of bankruptcy, Liddy told Congress that had AIG gone bankrupt and been put into receivership, the contracts that awarded those bonuses would have been void. Bankruptcy would have saved the taxpayers not only $165 million in bonuses, but also the latest $30 billion in AIG bailout. Liddy pointed this out to the Fed [Federal Reserve System] a month ago, according to Brad Sherman, Democrat of California, in the *Washington Post*.

Begging Barney Frank not to subpoena the names of the executives who got bonuses, Liddy read aloud a death threat from an outraged citizen who would like to strangle AIG execs with piano wire.

The Obama administration and congressional Democrats are responding to outpouring of anger.

But the truth is, the bonuses to greedy execs are just a sideshow. It's the government's willingness to give away hundreds of billions of dollars in yet another massive bailout that people should be shouting about.

8

It Is Necessary to Pay Bonuses to Wall Street Employees

Edward M. Liddy

Edward M. Liddy is the former chairman and chief executive officer of American International Group, Inc. (AIG).

While the American International Group, Inc. (AIG) has received federal government funds, the company is nonetheless required to continue to pay retention and corporate bonuses to employees. Many retention bonuses are contractual and it would be illegal to break those contracts. Also, corporate bonuses allow employers to retain the best employees. Still, AIG is committed to reducing bonuses in the future, especially in regard to grievous errors such as those that led to the company's financial collapse in 2008.

M r. [Treasury] Secretary [Timothy F. Geithner]:

Thank you for the open and frank conversation on Wednesday [in March 2009] regarding the compensation arrangements at AIG Financial Products and AIG [American International Group, Inc.] generally. I admit that the conversation was a difficult one for me.

I do not participate in any AIG bonus or retention program, have never attended a single AIG sales event or conference and, before September [2008], did not have any relationship with AIG. I was asked to serve by your predecessor in connection with the acquisition by the government of almost 80% of AIG's outstanding shares. My only goals are to have AIG repay, with interest, to the maximum extent possible, the assistance the American taxpayers have given it and to continue AIG's main insurance companies as strong, thriving businesses and contributors to the economy. My only stake is my reputation.

Retention Bonuses

In the first quarter of 2008, prior management took significant retention steps [bonuses issued to employees who remain with the company] at AIG Financial Products. These arrangements were designed at a time when AIG Financial Products was expected to have a significant, ongoing role at AIG, and guaranteed a minimum level of pay for both 2008 and 2009. (Due to losses at AIG Financial Products, a senior manager will receive about 43% of his 2007 expected level for 2008.) Some of these payments are coming due on March 15, and, quite frankly, AIG's hands are tied. Outside counsel has advised that these are legal, binding obligations of AIG, and there are serious legal, as well as business, consequences for not paying. Given the trillion-dollar portfolio at AIG Financial Products, retaining key traders and risk managers is critical to our goal of repayment. . . .

Needless to say, in the current circumstances, I do not like these arrangements and find it distasteful and difficult to recommend to you that we must proceed with them. With the benefit of hindsight, I would have designed these differently and at significantly lower levels. I am committed, however, to working within the existing arrangements to get the most out of them for AIG's constituencies. Honoring contractual commitments is at the heart of what we do in the insurance business. I cannot have our clients lose faith in our desire and ability to do just that.

We believe that there will be considerably greater flexibility to reduce contractual payments in respect of 2009, and AIG intends to use its best efforts to do so. It is expected that, over the course of the year, AIG Financial Products will sell certain businesses, employees will leave voluntarily or be terminated for cause and certain downsized employees will find new employment. In the first two cases, employees are no longer entitled to retention amounts from AIG; in particular, if AIG Financial Products sells certain books of business as planned, the employees related to these books will go with the sold businesses, and we intend to require the buyer to assume going-forward compensation payments. In the case of downsized employees who find new employment, their payments are reduced by earnings from their new employer. In addition, in foreign jurisdictions, AIG will have greater ability to negotiate with employees who are downsized.

Honoring contractual commitments is at the heart of what we do in the insurance business.

With all of these actions and other creative restructuring solutions, AIG hereby commits to use best efforts to reduce expected 2009 retention payments by at least 30%. We are also taking other significant steps to limit overall compensation at AIG Financial Products where we can. The 25 highest paid active-contract employees at AIG Financial Products have agreed to reduce their remaining 2009 salary to $1. Salaries for this group range up to $500,000, and the average salary is in excess of $270,000. The remaining 2009 salary of all other officers—that is, anyone with a title of associate vice president or higher—will be reduced by 10% (subject to local law requirements). In addition, other forms of non-cash compensation will be reduced or eliminated. Finally, AIG also is committed to seeking other ways to repay the American taxpayers for AIG Financial Products' retention payments.

Corporate Bonuses

You have also asked AIG to rethink our 2008 corporate bonus proposals. The proposals AIG originally submitted to you are part of a deliberate process, recommended by me and supported by the independent compensation committee of AIG's board of directors. We started with the additional compensation limits that AIG had already committed to—limits that were more extensive than those of any other recipient of TARP [Troubled Asset Relief Program] funds at the time—and weighed a variety of considerations appropriate to the goal of repayment and AIG's unique circumstances.

We cannot attract and retain the best and brightest talent to lead and staff the AIG businesses . . . if employees believe that their compensation is subject to continued and arbitrary adjustment by the U.S. Treasury.

Nevertheless, in response to your request, we are now proposing further changes to the 2008 corporate bonus proposals for senior partners that will better align their interests with AIG's restructuring efforts and the goal of repayment. As before, our Leadership Group (including me) will receive no 2008 year-end bonus.

I would not be doing my job if I did not directly advise you of my grave concern about the long-term consequences of the actions we are taking today. On the one hand, all of us at AIG recognize the environment in which we operate and the remonstrations of our President [Barack Obama] for a more restrained system of compensation for executives. On the other hand, we cannot attract and retain the best and brightest talent to lead and staff the AIG businesses—which are now being operated principally on behalf of the American taxpayers—if employees believe that their compensation is subject to continued and arbitrary adjustment by the U.S. Treasury.

My team and I will stand ready to do everything we can to work together with you to reach a resolution that is in the best interests of AIG and its stakeholders.

9

The Wealthy Profit at the Expense of the Poor and Middle Classes

Leslie Davis

Leslie Davis is a columnist for the Atlanta Mortgage Examiner.

A growing income disparity exists between the rich and the poor in the United States. This disparity creates a broader social problem. When wealth is concentrated in the hands of a few people, power within society is unequal. In the United States, the growth in the income gap has tarnished the idea of the American dream. Without good jobs, a home, and security, many Americans can no longer achieve this dream. The concentration of wealth has also led to a concentration of political power. As a result, the American political system serves the wealthy few.

As I read story after story about foreclosure, unemployment, the recession, health care, etc., I am frequently struck by the disparity in wealth and opportunity that exists in our country. It is often justified, dismissed or ignored.

Whereas we as a wealthy Western nation with a larger selection of toothpaste than most folks in the world have options for food, there is an ongoing problem with hunger, homelessness, lack of health care and inadequate education for many citizens of this country.

Wealth Concentration

In the United States, wealth is highly concentrated. As of 2004, the top 1% of households owned 34.3% of all privately held wealth, and the next 19% (the managerial, professional and small business stratum) had 50.3%, which means that just 20% of the people control 85% of the nation's wealth, leaving only 15% for the bottom 80% (wage and salary workers). In terms of financial wealth (total net worth less the value of one's home), the top 1% of households had a 42.2% share of the overall wealth. . . .

In the United States, wealth is highly concentrated.

In 2004, the average white household had 10 times as much total wealth as the average African American household and 21 times as much as the average Latino household. If we exclude home equity from the calculations and consider only financial wealth, the disparity becomes more alarming: 120:1 and 360:1, respectively. 69% of white families' wealth is in the form of their principal residence. For blacks and Hispanics, the figures are 97% and 98%, respectively. That data was generated prior to the housing bubble. The collapse of the housing market has impacted black and Latino households more dramatically, because the bulk of their wealth is invested in an asset losing value. If the analysts predicting further value declines and a decade of recovery are accurate, then black and Latino households have lost more wealth than white households due to the disparity in the home as a component of their overall financial wealth.

The Importance of Wealth

Wealth can be seen as a "resource" that can be utilized to exercise power via donations to political parties, payments to lobbyists and grants to experts, who are employed to think up new policies beneficial to the wealthy. Wealth is useful in shaping the general social environment to the benefit of the wealthy through hiring public relations firms or donating money to universities, museums, music halls and art galleries.

Certain kinds of wealth, such as stock ownership, allows the wealthy to access power through the control of corporations. Obviously, this has a major impact on how society and the economy function. The top 1%'s share of stock equity increased between 2001 and 2004. If the top 20% have 84% of the wealth, and 10% have 85% to 90% of the stocks, bonds, trust funds and business equity, that means that the U.S. is a power pyramid. It's challenging for the bottom 80%–90% to get organized and exercise much power in the absence of assets.

Certain kinds of wealth, such as stock ownership, allows the wealthy to access power through the control of corporations.

In American society, wealth and well-being are highly valued. The American dream is based on property ownership, high income, access to interesting and safe jobs, and access to health care that will extend longevity and quality of life. All of these "values" are unequally distributed amongst the population.

Unfair Wealth Distribution

When you evaluate the data regarding the distribution of wealth, it becomes evident that it is not "fair" and that opportunity distribution is not equitable. Whereas we laud meritocracy and the principles of equality in our country, the data indicates that inequality is increasing over time.

There was a period between the 1930s and 1970s where wealth distribution was more evenly distributed as a result of governmental regulation impeding the concentration of wealth after the market collapse that heralded the onset of the Great Depression. However, the trend towards a high concentration of wealth resumed in the late 1970s with governmental deregulation.

Whereas we laud meritocracy and the principles of equality in our country, the data indicates that inequality is increasing over time.

J. Bradford DeLong of the University of [California,] Berkeley did an interesting article regarding the robber barons of the last century and the distribution of wealth as it relates to economic growth. It is a lengthy article, but well worth reading for those interested in the topic.

The period since the mid-1970s has seen wealth concentration in the United States increase more rapidly than ever before, including during the heyday of industrialization in the final decades of the nineteenth century. Aggregate measures of wealth concentration today are greater than at any time since the election of Franklin D. Roosevelt in the Great Depression. They are within striking distance of the peak of wealth concentration reached during the Gilded Age.

The hostility of Roosevelt's New Deal to massive private concentrations of economic power was effective: The flow of new billionaires dried up, as the links between finance and industry that they had used to climb to the heights of fortune were cut.

Did the hostility of America's political and economic environment to billionaires between 1930 and 1980 harm the American economy? Did it slow the rate of economic growth by discouraging entrepreneurship? There is no quantitative evidence indicating that the political backlash against billionaires by Roosevelt's administration harmed the American economy.

Very great fortunes have three origins:

- *inheritance, plus a stock market boom.*

- *persuading the government to do your enterprise a truly massive favor.*

- *being at the right place at the right time: creating an enterprise of truly enormous social utility—and thereafter both retaining the market power to turn a large chunk of that extra social utility into firm profits, and retaining a sufficient ownership share and access to capital markets to turn capitalized firm profits into an enormous fortune.*

These causes of immense wealth have nothing to do with the determinants of the relative supplies of skilled and unskilled workers, or with the technological requirements of production. It makes me think that the overall level of wealth concentration is much more a "political" and a "cultural" phenomenon than an "economic" one: that we, through our political systems and our attitudes, have much more to do with the concentration of wealth than does the dance of factor supplies and technology-driven factor demands.

The years since 1980 have seen the return of the super-rich in the United States. Some of this is due to the great stock market boom of the past decade and a half, which has carried many of those who inherited their wealth and whose ancestors had never achieved "billionaire" status into the billionaire category. These are America's first true inherited aristocracy: the first generation of those with immense social and economic power who have inherited it.

The return of the super-rich is due to the blurring of the lines between financiers and corporate managers as the Depression-era order of American finance has fallen apart. It is once again possible to raise large sums of money and then direct them to suit one's own interest, rather than turning them over to salaried managers interested in perpetuating organizations.

Economic Scarcity

A couple hundred years ago a child raised in poverty taught himself to read from a handful of books he had access to as his family fell deeper into poverty. As an adult, he became a philosopher and a pioneer in the study of political economies. Despite his humble beginnings, Adam Smith became the father of modern economics. In his magnus opus, *The Wealth of Nations* [1776], he wrote about the rich of his day:

> They only select from the heap what is most precious and agreeable. They consume little more than the poor, and in spite of their natural selfishness and rapacity, though they mean only ... the gratification of their own vain and insatiable desires, they [inevitably] divide with the poor the produce of all their improvements. They are [thus] led by an invisible hand to make nearly the same distribution of the necessaries of life [as] ... had the earth been divided into equal portions.

Has the American dream become a utopian fantasy for 1% of our population while drifting beyond the reach of the rest of us?

Jobs are scarce. People are losing their houses at an alarming pace. Does it really matter to everyday Americans if the Wall Street stock hounds perceive economic recovery? If you are one of the 10%+ unemployed, does it look like economic recovery from where you are standing? For the small business owner struggling to keep the doors open and cutting back hours to avoid layoffs, speculation about economic improvement does nothing to increase sales this month. Given the political capital wielded by the wealthy, can the vast majority of Americans expect that the political machine will serve their interests? Has the American dream become a utopian fantasy for 1% of our population while drifting beyond the reach of the rest of us?

10

The Wealthy Should Pay Taxes at a Higher Rate

George Lakoff and Bruce Budner

George Lakoff was a senior fellow and founder and Bruce Budner was the executive director of the Rockridge Institute, a nonprofit, nonpartisan think tank focused on supporting progressive policy goals. The Rockridge Institute closed for lack of funds in April 2008.

The promise of progressive taxation is that those with more wealth are more able to contribute to the common good. In general, government serves to protect and empower its citizens, and tax money provides a nation's wealth. While conservatives argue that taxing the wealthy at a higher rate is unfair, they fail to consider who benefits the most from tax dollars. Tax revenues enable the legal system that protects intellectual property and contracts, for example. In addition, a nation's wealth supports a healthy banking system and stock market. All of these systems are essential for the expansion of wealth. Progressive taxation, then, is fair, and it is imperative for the United States to return to a more fair form of taxation.

At this time of year [April 2007] it seems there are only two things certain in life, taxes and anxiety about taxes. Instead of the perennial talk of a simplified tax form, how about a simplified understanding of the progressive values that underlie our tradition of progressive taxation?

Such an understanding won't move the tax deadline. But it might eliminate some of the anxiety. Understanding the hid-

George Lakoff and Bruce Budner, "Progressive Taxation: Some Hidden Truths," Rockridge Institute, April 15, 2007. Reproduced by permission of the authors.

den truths behind progressive taxation might also lead to more coherent—and more just—tax policies.

Progressive Taxation

Progressive taxation—taxing the wealthy at higher rates than the poor—is a moral issue. Like many moral issues, it sparks heated debate. The debate is borne of conflicting worldviews, values, and understandings of values. But as we at the Rockridge Institute have written, when progressives understand the values and ideas that underlie their positions on issues, they can articulate arguments authentically and with greater persuasive force. These arguments will appeal to those whom we call biconceptuals—the great majority of Americans whose worldviews borrow in various ways from both progressive and conservative values.

Progressive taxation—taxing the wealthy at higher rates than the poor—is a moral issue.

America's government has at least two fundamental functions, protection and empowerment. Protection includes the police, firefighters, emergency services, public health, the military, and so on. Empowerment includes the infrastructure needed for business and everyday life: roads, communications systems, water supplies, public education, the banking system for loans and economic stability, the SEC [Securities and Exchange Commission] for the stock market, the courts for enforcing contracts, air traffic control, support for basic science, our national parks and public buildings, and more. We are usually aware of protection. But the empowerment infrastructure, provided by taxes, is usually taken for granted, hidden, or ignored. Yet it is absolutely crucial, a fundamental truth about America and why America provides opportunity.

This is a basic truth. That is what framing [the study of thought] should be about: revealing truths and allowing us to reason using them.

Taxes as Common Wealth

Taxes are part of our common wealth, what we all share. Protection and empowerment serve the common good. Because of our common wealth, we are all protected and America's empowering infrastructure is available to all. That is a fundamental American value: The common wealth should serve the common good. It benefits everyone.

Citizens are financially responsible to maintain this common wealth. If we shirked this responsibility, we could not maintain our roads, fund our schools, protect ourselves from military threats, enforce our laws, and so on. Equally importantly, we could not create prosperity for ourselves, because we would have no protection of our intellectual property, no oversight of our markets, no means to enforce our contracts, no way to educate most of our children.

Taxes are part of our common wealth, what we all share.

Several main progressive values support the idea of progressive taxation. One is the belief that the common wealth should be used for the common good. Another is responsibility, the responsibility that citizens have to pay for the benefits we receive from our common wealth. And still another is fairness. These values intertwine on the question of progressive taxation.

Few people dispute this responsibility at some level. Disagreements generally arise over the amount and the relative apportionment of the responsibility. Differing concepts of fairness drive this debate. While many progressives say it is only fair that those who earn more pay a higher percentage of their earnings as taxes compared to those who have difficulty making ends meet, conservatives respond by asserting that it is unfair to "punish" the financially successful by making them pay more.

"Compound Empowerment"

An important point often lost in this debate is an appreciation that the common wealth, which our taxes create and sustain, empowers the wealthy in myriad ways to create their wealth. We call this *compound empowerment*—the compounded use of the common wealth by corporations, their investors, and other wealthy individuals.

Consider Bill Gates. He started Microsoft as a college dropout and has become the world's richest person. Though he has undoubtedly benefited from his unusual intelligence and business acumen, he could not have created or sustained his personal wealth without the common wealth. The legal system protected Microsoft's intellectual property and contracts. The tax-supported financial infrastructure enabled him to access capital markets and trade his stock in a market in which investors have confidence. He built his company with many employees educated in public schools and universities. Tax-funded research helped develop computer science and the Internet. Trade laws negotiated and enforced by the government protect his ability to sell his products abroad. These are but a few of the ways in which Mr. Gates' accumulation of wealth was empowered by the common wealth and by taxation.

As Warren Buffett famously observed, he likely couldn't have achieved his financial success had he been born in Bangladesh instead of the United States, because Bangladesh had no banking system and no stock market.

Ordinary people just drive on the highways; corporations send fleets of trucks. Ordinary people may get a bank loan for their mortgage; corporations borrow money to buy whole companies. Ordinary people rarely use the courts; most of the courts are used for corporate law and contract disputes. Corporations and their investors—those who have accumulated enough money beyond basic needs so they can invest—make much more use, compound use, of the empowering infrastructure provided by everybody's tax money.

The Obligation of the Wealthy

The wealthy have made greater use of the common good—they have been empowered by it in creating their wealth—and thus they have a greater moral obligation to sustain it. They are merely paying their debt to society in arrears and investing in future empowerment.

This is the fundamental truth that motivates progressive taxation.

It is a truth that undercuts conservative arguments about taxation. Taxes provide and maintain the protecting and empowering infrastructure that makes our income possible.

We need to return to a fair tax policy that recognizes financial responsibility incurred by the compound use of America's empowering infrastructure.

A Fair Tax Policy

Our tax forms hide this truth. They do not indicate the extent to which taxes have created and sustained the common wealth so you could earn what you have. They make it look like the empowering infrastructure was just put there by magic and that the government is taking money out of your pocket. The most likely truth is that, through the common wealth, America put more money in your pocket than it took out—by far.

But this situation is threatened by conservative tax policy. Through unfair cuts in taxes paid by the wealthy, through payment for the invasion and occupation of Iraq, and through borrowing abroad to pay for the tax cuts and Iraq, the common wealth is being drained and the infrastructure allowed to fall apart. We need to return to a fair tax policy that recognizes financial responsibility incurred by the compound use of America's empowering infrastructure.

11

Raising Taxes on the Wealthy Is Bad for the Economy

George F. Will

George F. Will is a Pulitzer Prize–winning columnist and a conservative political commentator. Will is a columnist for the Washington Post *and* Newsweek *magazine.*

Recently the House of Representatives has suggested raising taxes on the wealthy to pay for health insurance reform. The same Democrats who voted for this measure believe that the government—not the individual or private business—should create investment and provide charity. These policies, however, will result in an overall decrease in the United States' wealth. Taxing the rich, especially during the current recession, would be a mistake: American society, now more than ever, needs investment provided by the wealthy.

Tap a typical Democratic member of the House of Representatives on the knee with a rubber hammer and he or she will say: "Tax the rich!" If such a person, lounging in a lawn chair, is startled from a summer torpor by a cymbal crash, he or she will leap up exclaiming: "Tax the rich!" Forgive such people; they cannot help themselves. It is a reflex.

But people with only one idea really have no idea; they have only a mental default position. So, last week [in July 2009] the House decided to solve the problem of finding $1 trillion for health care by increasing taxes on the income of the 1.4 percent of taxpayers who already pay 45.2 percent of the income taxes—the rich, understood, for now, as those with annual household incomes of at least \$350,000. These people do a disproportionate share of society's investing and charitable giving, so there will be less of both if the House has its way.

Less of both would be an improvement, according to statists who think both should be done primarily by government rather than individuals, the better to engineer improved equality, understood as a more equal dependence of almost everyone on government for almost everything.

Policies, such as steeply progressive taxation, that are intended to increase equality are likely to decrease society's wealth.

Decreasing Society's Wealth

But there are unmentionable trade-offs. Richard Posner, senior lecturer at the University of Chicago Law School and judge on the U.S. Court of Appeals for the Second Circuit, says what no elected official dares to say: "As society becomes more competitive and more meritocratic, income inequality is likely to rise simply as a consequence of the underlying inequality— which is very great—between people that is due to differences in IQ, energy, health, social skills, character, ambition, physical attractiveness, talent, and luck." Hence policies, such as steeply progressive taxation, that are intended to increase equality are likely to decrease society's wealth. They reduce the role of merit in the allocation of social rewards—merit as markets measure it, in terms of value added to the economy.

It is, of course, possible to argue that the gain in equality of condition is worth the net loss in affluence. It is, however, telling that *no* public official actually makes that argument.

Today, in the midst of what history may remember as the Great Recession, it is especially risky to siphon away still more of the resources of the investor class. It is prudent to expect that business investment will have to play a larger role in fueling economic growth than it has played in the last quarter century. This is because private consumption may not soon be what it was between 1983 and 2008.

Speculating in the *Wilson Quarterly* about a "new normal," Martin Walker, a senior scholar at the Woodrow Wilson International Center for Scholars in Washington [D.C.], notes that for more than three decades after World War II, private consumption as a percentage of GDP [gross domestic product] varied within a narrow band, between 61 and 63 percent. In 1983, however, consumption began to rise, and reached 70 percent in 2007, fueled in part by $500 billion annually in home equity loans.

Today, in the midst of what history may remember as the Great Recession, it is especially risky to siphon away still more of the resources of the investor class.

Suppose the old, pre-1983 normal returns as the new normal. In 2007, personal consumption, at 70 percent of the $13.8 trillion GDP, was $9.7 trillion. Martin calculates that if it had been even at the upper end of the 1946–1983 norm, at 63 percent, 2007 consumption would have been *$1 trillion less.*

Financial Apocalypse

In 2007, Americans' savings rate was approximately zero. Today it is 7 percent of disposable income. Which is fine: Daniel Akst, a contributing editor of the *Wilson Quarterly*, notes that the noun "thrift" is etymologically related to the verb "thrive." That should, however, be a sobering thought to a nation in which last year more than half of all college students had at least four credit cards. The credit card is one of what Akst calls the four horsemen of the financial apocalypse.

The other three are the automobile, the television, and the shopping cart: Cars made possible population dispersal and large lots for large houses with lots of room for stuff. Television, the powerful marketer in the living room, made it unnecessary to imagine new stuff; it showed what might be bought with credit cards, which separated the pleasure of purchasing from the pain of paying. And, says Akst, the shopping cart, although unknown in traditional department stores (carts in Marshall Field? Heaven forfend), is suited to all-you-can-carry, buffet-style shopping at Wal-Mart and Target. Carts are necessities for hauling superfluities to the large car for the drive to the large house.

If the age of conspicuous consumption is behind us and conspicuous-nonconsumption—frugality chic? "Notice how I am trying not to be noticed"?—is upon us, heaven help us. Heaven had better, because the investor class, squeezed again and again, might be too anemic to provide the economic propulsion that used to come from consumers.

12

Raising State Taxes on the Wealthy Harms State Economies

Arthur Laffer and Stephen Moore

Arthur Laffer, often described as the father of supply-side economics, is the founder and chairman of Laffer Associates, an economic research and consulting firm. Stephen Moore is senior economics writer for the Wall Street Journal. *Laffer and Moore are the co-authors of the study* Rich States, Poor States.

Because of the recent economic crisis in the United States, many states seem to believe that raising taxes on the wealthy will help balance the budget. Studies have shown, however, that states with lower taxes create more jobs, and that many wealthy people will move—if tax rates are increased—to lower-tax states. Some commentators have argued that lower taxes will harm the quality of public education and other public services, though national test scores reveal this to be untrue. In order to compete in today's global economy, states must maintain low taxes to attract the wealthy.

With states facing nearly $100 billion in combined budget deficits this year, we're seeing more governors than ever proposing the Barack Obama solution to balancing the budget: Soak the rich. Lawmakers in California, Connecticut, Delaware, Illinois, Minnesota, New Jersey, New York and Oregon want to raise income tax rates on the top 1% or 2% or

5% of their citizens. New Illinois Gov. Patrick Quinn wants a 50% increase in the income tax rate on the wealthy because this is the "fair" way to close his state's gaping deficit.

Mr. Quinn and other tax-raising governors have been emboldened by recent studies by left-wing groups like the Center on Budget and Policy Priorities that suggest that "tax increases, particularly tax increases on higher-income families, may be the best available option." A recent letter to New York Gov. David Paterson signed by 100 economists advises the Empire State to "raise tax rates for high-income families right away."

Here's the problem for states that want to pry more money out of the wallets of rich people. It never works, because people, investment capital and businesses are mobile: They can leave tax-unfriendly states and move to tax-friendly states.

And the evidence that we discovered in our new study for the American Legislative Exchange Council, *Rich States, Poor States*, published in March, shows that Americans are more sensitive to high taxes than ever before. The tax differential between low-tax and high-tax states is widening, meaning that a relocation from high-tax California or Ohio, to no–income tax Texas or Tennessee, is all the more financially profitable both in terms of lower tax bills and more job opportunities.

> *Dozens of academic studies—old and new—have found clear and irrefutable statistical evidence that high state and local taxes repel jobs and businesses.*

Updating some research from Richard Vedder of Ohio University, we found that from 1998 to 2007, more than 1,100 people every day including Sundays and holidays moved from the nine highest income tax states such as California, New Jersey, New York and Ohio and relocated mostly to the nine tax-haven states with no income tax, including Florida, Nevada, New Hampshire and Texas. We also found that over these same years the no–income tax states created 89% more jobs and had 32% faster personal income growth than their high-tax counterparts.

Did the greater prosperity in low-tax states happen by chance? Is it coincidence that the two highest tax rate states in the nation, California and New York, have the biggest fiscal holes to repair? No. Dozens of academic studies—old and new—have found clear and irrefutable statistical evidence that high state and local taxes repel jobs and businesses.

Martin Feldstein, Harvard economist and former president of the National Bureau of Economic Research, co-authored a famous study in 1998 called *Can State Taxes Redistribute Income?* This should be required reading for today's state legislators. It concludes: "Since individuals can avoid unfavorable taxes by migrating to jurisdictions that offer more favorable tax conditions, a relatively unfavorable tax will cause gross wages to adjust. . . . A more progressive tax thus induces firms to hire fewer high-skilled employees and to hire more low-skilled employees."

More recently, Barry W. Poulson of the University of Colorado last year examined many factors that explain why some states grew richer than others from 1964 to 2004 and found "a significant negative impact of higher marginal tax rates on state economic growth." In other words, soaking the rich doesn't work. To the contrary, middle-class workers end up taking the hit.

Finally, there is the issue of whether high-income people move away from states that have high income tax rates. Examining IRS tax return data by state, E.J. McMahon, a fiscal expert at the Manhattan Institute, measured the impact of large income tax rate increases on the rich ($200,000 income or more) in Connecticut, which raised its tax rate in 2003 to 5% from 4.5%; in New Jersey, which raised its rate in 2004 to 8.97% from 6.35%; and in New York, which raised its tax rate in 2003 to 7.7% from 6.85%. Over the period 2002–2005, in each of these states the "soak the rich" tax hike was followed by a significant reduction in the number of rich people paying taxes in these states relative to the national average. Amazingly, these three states ranked 46th, 49th and 50th among all states in the percentage increase in wealthy tax filers in the years after they tried to soak the rich.

This result was all the more remarkable given that these were years when the stock market boomed and Wall Street gains were in the trillions of dollars. Examining data from a 2008 Princeton study on the New Jersey tax hike on the wealthy, we found that there were 4,000 missing half-millionaires in New Jersey after that tax took effect. New Jersey now has one of the largest budget deficits in the nation.

Since many rich people also tend to be successful business owners, jobs leave with them or they never arrive in the first place.

We believe there are three unintended consequences from states raising tax rates on the rich. First, some rich residents sell their homes and leave the state; second, those who stay in the state report less taxable income on their tax returns; and third, some rich people choose not to locate in a high-tax state. Since many rich people also tend to be successful business owners, jobs leave with them or they never arrive in the first place. This is why high income-tax states have such a tough time creating net new jobs for low-income residents and college graduates.

Those who disapprove of tax competition complain that lower state taxes only create a zero-sum competition where states "race to the bottom" and cut services to the poor as taxes fall to zero. They say that tax cutting inevitably means lower quality schools and police protection as lower tax rates mean starvation of public services.

They're wrong, and New Hampshire is our favorite illustration. The Live Free or Die State has no income or sales tax, yet it has high-quality schools and excellent public services. Students in New Hampshire public schools achieve the fourth-highest test scores in the nation—even though the state spends about $1,000 a year less per resident on state and local government than the average state and, incredibly, $5,000 less per person than New York. And on the other side of the ledger, California in 2007 had the highest-paid classroom teachers in the nation, and yet the Golden State had the second-lowest test scores.

Or consider the fiasco of New Jersey. In the early 1960s, the state had no state income tax and no state sales tax. It was a rapidly growing state attracting people from everywhere and running budget surpluses. Today its income and sales taxes are among the highest in the nation yet it suffers from perpetual deficits and its schools rank among the worst in the nation—much worse than those in New Hampshire. Most of the massive infusion of tax dollars over the past 40 years has simply enriched the public-employee unions in the Garden State. People are fleeing the state in droves.

The Live Free or Die State [New Hampshire] has no income or sales tax, yet it has high-quality schools and excellent public services.

One last point: States aren't simply competing with each other. As Texas Gov. Rick Perry recently told us, "Our state is competing with Germany, France, Japan and China for business. We'd better have a pro-growth tax system or those American jobs will be outsourced." Gov. Perry and Texas have the jobs and prosperity model exactly right. Texas created more new jobs in 2008 than all other 49 states combined. And Texas is the only state other than Georgia and North Dakota that is cutting taxes this year.

The Texas economic model makes a whole lot more sense than the New Jersey model, and we hope the politicians in California, Delaware, Illinois, Minnesota and New York realize this before it's too late.

13

The Health Care System Favors the Wealthy and Harms the Poor

Guy Adams

Guy Adams is the Independent's *correspondent in Los Angeles.*

While a number of commentators have argued that nothing is wrong with the American system of health care, a basic fact remains: Wealthy Americans have access to quality health care while many poorer Americans do not. This point became clear when the organization Remote Area Medical Volunteer Corps set up a massive clinic in the Los Angeles Forum in the summer of 2009. Thousands of uninsured Americans crowded the stadium for treatment, many seeking aid for long-neglected maladies. The clinic served as a reminder that 50 million Americans do not have health care insurance and that a new health care system is needed.

They came in their thousands, queuing through the night to secure one of the coveted wristbands offering entry into a strange parallel universe where medical care is a free and basic right and not an expensive luxury. Some of these Americans had walked miles simply to have their blood pressure checked, some had slept in their cars in the hope of getting an eye test or a mammogram, others had brought their children for immunisations that could end up saving their life.

In the week that Britain's National Health Service [NHS] was held aloft by Republicans as an "evil and Orwellian" ex-

Guy Adams, "The Brutal Truth About America's Healthcare," *The Independent*, August 15, 2009. Copyright © 2009 Independent Newspapers (UK) Ltd. Reproduced by permission.

ample of everything that is wrong with free healthcare, these extraordinary scenes in Inglewood, California, yesterday [14 August 2009] provided a sobering reminder of exactly why President Barack Obama is trying to reform the US system.

Free Healthcare, American Style

The LA [Los Angeles] Forum, the arena that once hosted sell-out Madonna concerts, has been transformed—for eight days only—into a vast field hospital. In America, the offer of free healthcare is so rare that news of the magical medical kingdom spread rapidly and long lines of prospective patients snaked around the venue for the chance of getting everyday treatments that many British people take for granted.

In the first two days, more than 1,500 men, women and children received free treatments worth $503,000 (£304,000). Thirty dentists pulled 471 teeth; 320 people were given standard issue spectacles; 80 had mammograms; dozens more had acupuncture, or saw kidney specialists. By the time the makeshift medical centre leaves town on Tuesday, staff expect to have dispensed $2m [million] worth of treatments to 10,000 patients.

By the time the makeshift medical centre leaves town ..., staff expect to have dispensed $2m [million] worth of treatments to 10,000 patients.

The gritty district of Inglewood lies just a few miles from the palm-lined streets of Beverly Hills and the bright lights of Hollywood, but is a world away. And the residents who had flocked for the free medical care, courtesy of mobile charity Remote Area Medical [Volunteer Corps], bore testament to the human cost of the healthcare mess that President Obama is attempting to fix.

Living Without Healthcare

Christine Smith arrived at 3 A.M. in the hope of seeing a dentist for the first time since she turned 18. That was almost eight years ago. Her need is obvious and pressing: 17 of her teeth are rotten; some have large visible holes in them. She is living in constant pain and has been unable to eat solid food for several years.

"I had a gastric bypass in 2002, but it went wrong, and stomach acid began rotting my teeth. I've had several jobs since, but none with medical insurance, so I've not been able to see a dentist to get it fixed," she told the *Independent*. "I've not been able to chew food for as long as I can remember. I've been living on soup, and noodles, and blending meals in a food mixer. I'm in constant pain. Normally, it would cost $5,000 to fix it. So if I have to wait a week to get treated for free, I'll do it. This will change my life."

Along the hall, Liz Cruise was one of scores of people waiting for a free eye exam. She works for a major supermarket chain but can't afford the $200 a month that would be deducted from her salary for insurance. "It's a simple choice: pay my rent, or pay my healthcare. What am I supposed to do?" she asked. "I'm one of the working poor: people who do work but can't afford healthcare and are ineligible for any free healthcare or assistance. I can't remember the last time I saw a doctor."

50 Million Without Healthcare

Although the Americans spend more on medicine than any nation on earth, there are an estimated 50 million with no health insurance at all. Many of those who have jobs can't afford coverage, and even those with standard policies often find it doesn't cover commonplace procedures. California's unemployed—who rely on Medicaid—had their dental care axed last month.

Julie Shay was one of the many, waiting to slide into a dentist's chair where teeth were being drilled in full view of passersby. For years, she has been crossing over the Mexican border to get her teeth done on the cheap in Tijuana. But recently, the US started requiring citizens returning home from Mexico to produce a passport (previously all you needed was a driver's license), and so that route is now closed. Today she has two abscesses and is in so much pain she can barely sleep. "I don't have a passport, and I can't afford one. So my husband and I slept in the car to make sure we got seen by a dentist. It sounds pathetic, but I really am that desperate."

Although the Americans spend more on medicine than any nation on earth, there are an estimated 50 million with no health insurance at all.

"You'd think, with the money in this country, that we'd be able to look after people's health properly," she said. "But the truth is that the rich, and the insurance firms, just don't realise what we are going through, or simply don't care. Look around this room and tell me that America's healthcare don't need fixing."

President Obama's healthcare plans had been a central plank of his first-term programme, but his reform package has taken a battering at the hands of Republican opponents in recent weeks. As the Democrats have failed to coalesce around a single, straightforward proposal, their rivals have seized on public hesitancy over "socialised medicine" and now the chance of far-reaching reform is in doubt.

Most damaging of all has been the tide of vociferous right-wing opponents whipping up scepticism at town hall meetings that were supposed to soothe doubts. In Pennsylvania this week, Senator Arlen Specter was greeted by a crowd of 1,000 at a venue designed to accommodate only 250, and of the 30 selected speakers at the event, almost all were hostile.

The Public Service Ethos

The packed bleachers in the LA Forum tell a different story. The mobile clinic has been organised by the remarkable Remote Area Medical. The charity usually focuses on the rural poor, although they worked in New Orleans after Hurricane Katrina [in 2005]. Now they are moving into more urban venues, this week's event in Los Angeles is believed to be the largest free healthcare operation in the country.

Doctors, dentists and therapists volunteer their time, and resources, to the organisation. To many US medical professionals, it offers a rare opportunity to plug into the public service ethos on which their trade was supposedly founded. "People come here who haven't seen a doctor for years. And we're able to say 'Hey, you have this, you have this, you have this'," said Dr Vincent Anthony, a kidney specialist volunteering five days of his team's time. "It's hard work, but incredibly rewarding. Healthcare needs reform, obviously. There are so many people falling through the cracks, who don't get care. That's why so many are here."

[The August 2009 Remote Area Medical] event in Los Angeles is believed to be the largest free healthcare operation in the country.

Ironically, given this week's transatlantic spat over the NHS, Remote Area Medical was founded by an Englishman: Stan Brock. The 72-year-old former public schoolboy, Taekwondo black belt, and one-time presenter of *Wild Kingdom*, one of America's most popular animal TV shows, left the celebrity gravy train in 1985 to, as he puts it, "make people better".

Today, Brock has no money, no income, and no bank account. He spends 365 days a year at the charity events, sleeping on a small rolled-up mat on the floor and living on a diet made up entirely of porridge and fresh fruit. In some quarters, he has been described, without too much exaggeration, as a living saint.

A Benchmark for U.S. Healthcare

Though anxious not to interfere in the potent healthcare debate, Mr Brock said yesterday that he, and many other professionals, believes the NHS should provide a benchmark for the future of US healthcare.

"Back in 1944, the UK government knew there was a serious problem with lack of healthcare for 49.7 million British citizens, of which I was one, so they said 'Hey Mr [Aneurin] Nye Bevan, you're the Minister of Health . . . go fix it'. And so came the NHS. Well, fast-forward now 66 years, and we've got about the same number of people, about 49 million people, here in the US, who don't have access to healthcare."

"I've been very conservative in my outlook for the whole of my life. I've been described as being about 90,000 miles to the right of Attila the Hun. But I think one reaches the reality that something doesn't work. . . . In this country something has to be done. And as a proud member of the US community but a loyal British subject to the core, I would say that if Britain could fix it in 1944, surely we could fix it here in America."

14

The Wealthy Are Monopolizing Prime Living Space

Barbara Ehrenreich

Barbara Ehrenreich is an activist and an award-winning author and journalist. She has written numerous nonfiction books, including Nickel and Dimed: On (Not) Getting by in America *and* Bait and Switch: The (Futile) Pursuit of the American Dream. *The following essay was adapted from her book* This Land Is Their Land: Reports from a Divided Nation.

There is an adage that states, "If a place is truly beautiful, you can't afford to be there." As many prime locations have become fashionable, rich Americans have monopolized the landscape. Once the rich arrive in a given area, ordinary Americans can no longer afford housing or even dining at local restaurants. Even the individuals who work in these resort towns must live in less expensive neighboring towns. In effect, the rich are monopolizing America's prime real estate.

I took a little vacation recently—nine hours in Sun Valley, Idaho, before an evening speaking engagement. The sky was deep blue, the air crystalline, the hills green and not yet on fire. Strolling out of the Sun Valley Lodge, I found a tiny tourist village, complete with Swiss-style bakery, multistar restaurant and "opera house." What luck—the boutiques were displaying outdoor racks of summer clothing on sale! Nature and commerce were conspiring to make this the perfect micro-vacation.

But as I approached the stores, things started to get a little sinister—maybe I had wandered into a movie set or Paris Hilton's closet?—because even at a 60-percent discount, I couldn't find a sleeveless cotton shirt for less than $100. These items shouldn't have been outdoors; they should have been in locked glass cases. Then I remembered the general rule, which has been in effect since sometime in the 1990s: If a place is truly beautiful, you can't afford to be there. All right, I'm sure there are still exceptions—a few scenic spots not yet eaten up by mansions. But they're going fast.

Transforming the Landscape

About ten years ago, for example, a friend and I rented a snug, inexpensive one-bedroom house in Driggs, Idaho, just over the Teton Range from wealthy Jackson Hole, Wyoming. At that time, Driggs was where the workers lived, driving over the Teton Pass every day to wait tables and make beds on the stylish side of the mountains. The point is, we low-rent folks got to wake up to the same scenery the rich people enjoyed and hike along the same pine-shadowed trails.

But the money was already starting to pour into Driggs—Paul Allen of Microsoft, August Busch III of Anheuser-Busch, [actor] Harrison Ford—transforming family potato farms into vast dynastic estates. I haven't been back, but I understand Driggs has become another unaffordable Jackson Hole. Where the wait staff and bed makers live today I do not know.

I witnessed this kind of deterioration up close in Key West, Florida, where I first went in 1986, attracted not only by the turquoise waters and frangipani-scented nights but by the fluid, egalitarian social scene. At a typical party you might find literary stars like Alison Lurie, Annie Dillard and Robert Stone, along with commercial fishermen, waitresses and men who risked their lives diving for treasure (once a major blue-collar occupation). Then, at some point in the '90s, the rich started pouring in. You'd see them on the small planes coming down from Miami—taut-skinned, linen-clad and impatient. They drove house prices into the seven-figure range. They encouraged restaurants to charge upward of $30 for an entree. They tore down working-class tiki bars to make room for their waterfront "condotels."

Stealing Beauty and Pleasure

Of all the crimes of the rich, the aesthetic deprivation of the rest of us may seem to be the merest misdemeanor. Many of them owe their wealth to the usual tricks: squeezing their employees, overcharging their customers and polluting any land they're not going to need for their third or fourth homes. Once they've made (or inherited) their fortunes, the rich can bid up the price of goods that ordinary people also need— housing, for example. Gentrification is dispersing the urban poor into overcrowded suburban ranch houses, while billionaires' horse farms displace rural Americans into trailer homes. Similarly, the rich can easily fork over annual tuitions of $50,000 and up, which has helped make college education a privilege of the upper classes.

There are other ways, too, that the rich are robbing the rest of us of beauty and pleasure. As the bleachers in stadiums and arenas are cleared to make way for skybox "suites" costing more than $100,000 for a season, going out to a ball game has become prohibitively expensive for the average family. At the other end of the cultural spectrum, superrich collectors have driven up the price of artworks, leading museums to charge ever-rising prices for admission.

Extreme wealth is ... a social problem, and the superrich have become a burden on everyone else.

It shouldn't be a surprise that the Pew Research Center [for the People & the Press] finds happiness to be unequally distributed, with 50 percent of people earning more than

$150,000 a year describing themselves as "very happy," compared with only 23 percent of those earning less than $20,000. When nations are compared, inequality itself seems to reduce well-being, with some of the most equal nations—Iceland and Norway—ranking highest, according to the UN's [United Nations'] Human Development Index. We are used to thinking that poverty is a "social problem" and wealth is only something to celebrate, but extreme wealth is also a social problem, and the superrich have become a burden on everyone else.

Plutocratic Takeover

If Edward O. Wilson is right about "biophilia"—an innate human need to interact with nature—there may even be serious mental health consequences to letting the rich hog all the good scenery. I know that if I don't get to see vast expanses of water, 360-degree horizons and mountains piercing the sky for at least a week or two of the year, chronic, cumulative claustrophobia sets in. According to evolutionary psychologist Nancy Etcoff, the need for scenery is hardwired into us. "People like to be on a hill, where they can see a landscape. And they like somewhere to go where they can *not* be seen themselves," she told *Harvard Magazine* last year. "That's a place desirable to a predator who wants to avoid becoming prey." We also like to be able to see water (for drinking), low-canopy trees (for shade) and animals (whose presence signals that a place is habitable).

Ultimately, the plutocratic takeover of rural America has a downside for the wealthy too. The more expensive a resort town gets, the farther its workers have to commute to keep it functioning. And if your heart doesn't bleed for the dishwasher or landscaper who commutes two to four hours a day, at least shed a tear for the wealthy vacationer who gets stuck in the ensuing traffic. It's bumper to bumper westbound out of Telluride, Colorado, every day at 5, or eastbound on Route 1 out of Key West, for the Lexuses as well as the beat-up old pickup trucks.

Or a place may simply run out of workers. Monroe County, which includes Key West, has seen more than 2,000 workers leave since the 2000 Census, a loss the *Los Angeles Times* calls "a body blow to the service-oriented economy of a county with only 75,000 residents and 2.25 million overnight visitors a year." Among those driven out by rents of more than $1,600 for a one-bedroom apartment are many of Key West's wait staff, hotel housekeepers, gardeners, plumbers and handymen. No matter how much money you have, everything takes longer—from getting a toilet fixed to getting a fish sandwich at Pepe's [Cafe].

Ultimately, the plutocratic takeover of rural America has a downside for the wealthy too.

This Land Is Their Land

Then there's the elusive element of charm, which quickly drains away in a uniform population of multimillionaires. The Hamptons had their fishermen. Key West still advertises its "characters"—sun-bleached, weather-beaten misfits who drifted down for the weather or to escape some difficult situation on the mainland. But the fishermen are long gone from the Hamptons and disappearing from Cape Cod. As for Key West's characters—with the traditional little conch houses once favored by shrimpers flipped into million-dollar second homes, these human sources of local color have to be prepared to sleep with the scorpions under the highway overpass.

In Telluride even a local developer is complaining about the lack of affordable housing. "To have a real town," he told the *Financial Times*, "Telluride needs some locals hanging out"—in old-fashioned diners, for example, where you don't have to speak Italian to order a cup of coffee.

When I was a child, I sang "America the Beautiful" and meant it. I was born in the Rocky Mountains and raised, at various times, on the coasts. The Big Sky, the rolling surf, the jagged, snowcapped mountains—all this seemed to be my birthright. But now I flinch when I hear Woody Guthrie's line "This land was made for you and me." Somehow, I don't think it was meant to be sung by a chorus of hedge fund operators.

15

The Addictive Striving for Wealth Has Negative Social Repercussions

Peter C. Whybrow

Peter C. Whybrow is a psychiatrist and neurologist. He has written several books including American Mania: When More Is Not Enough.

In contemporary times, it seems that few limits have been placed on the desires of the American consumer. Americans have accepted affluence as though a birthright, believing that real estate and financial markets would continue to expand. During the recent economic crisis, however, it has become obvious that the American system has limits. In an endless effort to acquire more, Americans have lost track of the original American dream founded in personal achievement. Instead of making Americans happy, the acquisition of consumer goods and pursuit of wealth have left many dissatisfied.

"It's called the American dream," George Carlin lamented shortly before his death, "because you have to be asleep to believe it." Too bad for the rest of us that George and his signature satire haven't been around for the wake-up call of the current market meltdown. After all, George Carlin knew something about the dangers of addiction from firsthand experience. He understood earlier than most that the debt-fueled consumptive frenzy that has gripped the American

Peter C. Whybrow, "Dangerously Addictive," *The Chronicle of Higher Education*, March 13, 2009. Copyright © 2009 by *The Chronicle of Higher Education*. Reproduced by permission from the author.

psyche for the past two decades was a nightmare in the making—a seductive, twisted and commercially conjured version of the American dream that now threatens our environmental, individual and civic health.

The United States is the quintessential trading nation and for the past quarter-century we have worshiped the "free" market as an ideology rather than for what it is—a natural product of human social evolution and a set of economic tools with which to construct a just and equitable society. Under the spell of this ideology and the false promise of instant riches America's immigrant values of thrift, prudence and community concern—traditionally the foundation of the dream—have been hijacked by an all-consuming self-interest. The astonishing appetite of the American consumer now determines some 70 percent of all economic activity in the US. And yet in this land of opportunity and material comfort—where we enjoy the 12-inch dinner plate, the 32-ounce soda, and the 64-inch TV screen—more and more citizens feel time starved, overworked and burdened by debt. Epidemic rates of obesity, anxiety, depression and family dysfunction are accepted as the norm.

The astonishing appetite of the American consumer now determines some 70 percent of all economic activity in the US.

It is the paradox of modernity that as choice and material prosperity increase health and personal satisfaction decline. This is now an accepted truth. And yet it is the rare American who manages to step back from the hedonic treadmill long enough to savor his or her good fortune. Indeed, for most of us, regardless of what we have, we want more, and we want it now. The roots of this conundrum—of this addictive striving—are to be found in our evolutionary history. As creatures of the natural world, having evolved under conditions of danger and scarcity, we are by instinct reward-seeking animals that discount the future in favor of the immediate present. As a species, we have no familiarity with the seductive prosperity and material riches that exists in America today. A novel experience, it is both compelling and confusing.

Three Brains in One

Brain systems of immediate reward were a vital survival adaptation millennia ago when finding a fruit tree was a rare delight and dinner had a habit of running away or flying out of reach. But living now in relative abundance, when the whole world is a shopping mall and our appetites are no longer constrained by limited resources, our craving for reward—be that for money, the fat and sugar of fast food, or for the novel gadgetry of modern technology—has become a liability and a hunger that has no bounds. Our nature has no built-in braking system. More is never enough.

That the human animal is a curiosity-driven pleasure seeker easily seduced is of no surprise to the behavioral neuroscientist. It is clearly established that "overloading" the brain's ancient reward circuits with excessive stimulation—through drugs, novel experience, or unlimited choice—will trigger craving and insatiable desire. Brain anatomy helps us understand why this is so.

Our nature has no built-in braking system. More is never enough.

The human brain is a hybrid: an evolved hierarchy of three-brains-in-one. A primitive "lizard" brain, designed millennia ago for survival, lies at its core and cradles the roots of the ancient dopamine reward pathways. When the dinosaurs still roamed, around this reptilian pith there evolved the limbic cortex—literally the "border crust"—of the early mammalian brain, which is the root of kinship behavior and nurturance. The evolution of mammalian species is marked by a continuous expansion of this cortex, with the pre-frontal lobes of the human brain—the powerful information processing or "executive" brain that distinguishes *Homo sapiens* within the primate lineage—emerging only recently, within the last two hundred thousand years.

With the three brains working in harmony the human animal has extraordinary adaptive advantage, as is evident from the success we have achieved as a species. Through a process of continuous learning—orchestrated by the executive brain—the risks and rewards inherent in changing circumstance are carefully assessed and the personal and social consequence of what we do is remembered to future benefit. But there is a catch. Despite our superior intelligence, as in all animals, we remain driven by our ancient desires. Desire is as vital as breathing. Indeed, in human experience, when desire is lost we call it anhedonia—or depression—and consider it an illness. But, as George Carlin understood, the flip side of this is that when the brain's reward circuits are overloaded or unconstrained, then desire can turn to craving and to an addictive greed that co-opts executive analysis and common sense.

Marketing Desire

All this is important when considering market behavior, for in the marketplace it is desire that fuels the vital engines of commerce—self-interest, novelty seeking and social ambition. It was Adam Smith—the eighteenth-century Scottish philosopher and capitalism's patron saint—that first cogently argued the value of harnessing what he called "self-love" (instinctual self-interest) within the give and take of a market framework to create a self-regulating economic order. Although it was well recognized that the human creature left unchecked has a propensity for greed, Smith argued that in a free society overweening self-interest is constrained by the wish to be loved by others (the limbic brain's drive for attachment) and by the "social sentiment" (empathic and commonsense behavior) that is learned by living in community.

Therefore, with the adoption of a few rules—such as honesty in competition, respect for private property, and the ability to exchange goods for money—personal desire can be safely liberated to prime the engines of economic growth. Self-love will be simultaneously molded to the common good by the complex personal relationships and the social order in which the "free" market operates; self-interest will ultimately serve the common interest. And indeed, experience tells us that locally capitalized neighborhood markets do sustain their own rational order founded as they are upon an interlocking system of self-interested exchange.

But Smith lived before the invention of the megacorporation, before instant global communication, and before the double cheeseburger and hedge funds. Today the tethers that once bound self-interest and social concern into closely knit economic communities, and which gave us Adam Smith's enduring metaphor of an "invisible hand" balancing market behavior, have been weakened by an intrusive mercantilism that never sleeps.

Since the 1950s, across the globe rapidly advancing technologies have removed the physical limitations once placed upon human activity by darkness, sea and distance thus diminishing the natural barriers to free market exchange. The United States, as a great trading nation, applauded these advances and sought to drive economic growth further by limiting government regulation of market practice as prescribed by economist Milton Friedman and the Chicago school [of economics]. Thus beginning in the late 1980s, as the Soviet Union crumbled and the Internet was commercialized, Smith's engines of economic growth—self-interest, curiosity and social ambition—were supercharged and placed in high gear with the conviction that Homo economicus, a presumed rational being, was capable of self-policing. Freed of constraint, markets would magically regulate themselves delivering to the American people an ever-increasing prosperity. With a bright future ahead, credit laws were relaxed and borrowing encouraged. The American dream was no longer a promise based upon old notions of toil and patience: It was immediate and material.

An Unsustainable Dream

We had perfected the consumer-driven society. The idea was simple and irresistible. It tapped deep into the nation's mythology and for a brief moment, during the exuberant years of the dot-com bubble, the dream was made material. Vast shopping malls proclaimed prosperity throughout the land. Horatio Alger's story was once again our story—the American story—but this time on steroids. Temptation was everywhere. And true to our instinctual origins, we were soon focused on immediate gratification ignoring future consequence. Shopping became the national pastime. Throwing caution to the wind, at all levels of our society we hungered for more—more money, more power, more food and more stuff.

It was a dream dangerously addictive, and one unsustainable. America's productivity per person per hour is comparable to that of most European nations but our material consumption per capita is greater by one-third. We finance the difference by working longer hours, sleeping less, cutting back on vacations, neglecting our families and by taking on debt—massive amounts of debt. Before 1985 American consumers saved on average about 9% of their disposable income but by 2005 the comparable savings rate was zero as mortgage, credit card and other consumer debt rose to 127% of disposable income. With Uncle Sam similarly awash in red ink, America had transformed itself from the world's bank to a debtor nation. The invisible hand had lost its grip.

The financial meltdown that began as the "subprime" mortgage crisis has finally brought home the inherent dangers of our reward-driven, shortsighted behavior. As the post-dot-com housing bubble inflated, both Wall Street financiers and ordinary Americans began to believe that real estate values could never fall. With prices skyrocketing at 20% each year, the family home was mistaken for a piggy bank—as just another asset to borrow against when struggling to finance an overstretched lifestyle. With zero down payment, adjustable interest rates and deregulated borrowing practices the challenge became, as George Dyson the historian has puckishly observed, "whether you can live in a house you've paid nothing for and spend it at the same time."

The conflict between seeking fame and fortune and the corrupting power of money is a perennial source of fascination in America.

But as we are now experiencing, the worst was yet to come. As part of the scramble toward "freeing" the market, in 2004 America's big investment banks had become exempt from Depression-era regulations that specified the capital reserves that must be held against losses. Instinctual desire, abetted by its wily cousin speculation, soon became greed. Avarice was rampant as the skill and analytic powers of the executive brain were placed in thrall to the lizard. Clever people were now manipulating money for money's sake. Mortgage-backed securities, credit derivatives, default obligations and other mysterious financial instruments designed to limit risk were packaged and repackaged to create unknown trillions of imaginary wealth. Homo economicus had been too clever by half. In reality, when the meltdown began, few people—even the financial gurus—truly understood what was happening. Caught in a web of our own creation, we first had fooled ourselves about the risks involved, and then the instruments we had created had fooled us. With the nation's financial system at the brink of disaster we found ourselves rudely awake.

A New American Dream

The conflict between seeking fame and fortune and the corrupting power of money is a perennial source of fascination in America. As I write this [in March 2009], *Road Show*, the much-repackaged story by [Stephen] Sondheim and [John] Weidman of the Mizner brothers and their get-rich-quick schemes, has opened in New York. The characters of Addison, the flapper-age dreamer who helped define the architectural vision of Florida's Palm Beach and Boca Raton, and Wilson, his manipulative huckster brother, together embody the striving that many Americans find irresistible—the urge to act out the dream in material representation.

But dreams are more than things material. Dreams cannot be packaged and placed on sale in the shopping mall. The American dream is not to be found in a new refrigerator, or a 64-inch TV screen, for as reward-driven creatures we quickly grow tired of such novelties. No, dreaming is a state of mind that binds the brain in harmony. For each of us our dreams are an evolving work of the imagination, built upon an elusive inner reality that is shaped by emotion and experience—an intuitive sense of future possibility that binds instinct and hope with commonsense analysis. As a guiding metaphor, the dream holds a unique place in American culture and it will continue to do so. This is because while the American Constitution is grounded in the Enlightenment and draws upon a faith in human reason, to dream is part of the émigré package, integral to our never-ending search for El Dorado [a legendary lost city of gold]. In our self-selection Americans are different: a migrant people defined by movement and change. By temperament we tend toward restlessness, optimism, curiosity, risk-taking and entrepreneurship—just as Alexis de Tocqueville described in *Democracy in America*, in 1831. It is these same qualities of mind that kindled the novus ordo seclorum—the "new order of the ages"—that was the dream of the Founding Fathers and is proclaimed still on the back of each US one dollar bill.

Somewhere along the road to affluence, caught up in the excitement of global markets, a virtual world of electronic wizardry and immediate material reward, America has lost sight of those founding hopes and dreams. What is the purpose of the journey in this land of opportunity when individual social mobility lags behind that of Europe, when 45 million souls are without health insurance and when our educational system is badly broken? Now with reality challenging the laissez-faire ideology of recent decades we have the opportunity to take stock with a renewed self-awareness, to curb our addictive striving and to reach beyond immediate reward to craft a vigorous, equitable and sustainable market society— one where technology and profit serve as instruments in achieving the good life and are not confused with the good life itself. The dream that material markets will ultimately deliver social perfection and human happiness is an illusion. Perfection does not exist in nature. Nature is infinitely more pragmatic. In nature it's all a matter of dynamic fit—of living creatures striving for balance with their surroundings. [Author] Anaïs Nin put it well: "The dream is always running ahead ... to catch up with it, to live for a moment in unison with it, that is the miracle." George Carlin would have agreed.

Organizations to Contact

The editors have compiled the following list of organizations concerned with the issues debated in this book. The descriptions are derived from materials provided by the organizations. All have publications or information available for interested readers. The list was compiled on the date of publication of the present volume; the information provided here may change. Be aware that many organizations take several weeks or longer to respond to inquiries, so allow as much time as possible.

Adbusters Media Foundation
1243 West Seventh Avenue, Vancouver
British Columbia   V6H 1B7
    Canada
(604) 736-9401 • fax: (604) 737-6021
e-mail: info@adbusters.org
Web site: www.adbusters.org

Adbusters Media Foundation is a network of artists, activists, writers, and other people who want to build a new social activist movement. The organization publishes *Adbusters* magazine, which explores the negative impact that commercialism has on physical and cultural environments. Spoof ads and information on political action are available on its Web site.

American Enterprise Institute for Public Policy Research (AEI)
1150 Seventeenth Street NW, Washington, DC   20036
(202) 862-5800 • fax: (202) 862-7177
Web site: www.aei.org

The American Enterprise Institute for Public Policy Research sponsors research and provides commentary on a wide variety of issues, including economics, social welfare, and government tax and regulatory policies. It publishes the bimonthly magazine *American Enterprise* and the *AEI Newsletter*.

Brookings Institution

1775 Massachusetts Avenue NW, Washington, DC   20036
(202) 797-6000 • fax: (202) 797-6004
e-mail: brookinfo@brookings.edu
Web site: www.brookings.edu

Founded in 1927, the Brookings Institution is a think tank that conducts research and education in foreign policy, economics, government, and the social sciences. Its Economic Studies program focuses on economic policy issues in the United States and around the world. Publications include the book *After the Crash: The Future of Finance*, and its Web site features papers, videos, and podcasts.

Cato Institute

1000 Massachusetts Avenue NW
Washington, DC   20001-5403
(202) 842-0200 • fax: (202) 842-3490
e-mail: cato@cato.org
Web site: www.cato.org

The Cato Institute is a nonpartisan public policy research foundation dedicated to limiting the role of government and protecting free markets and individual liberties. It publishes the quarterly magazine *Regulation*, the bimonthly *Cato Policy Report*, and numerous policy papers and articles.

Center for a New American Dream

6930 Carroll Avenue, Suite 900, Takoma Park, MD   20912
(301) 891-3683
e-mail: newdream@newdream.org
Web site: www.newdream.org

The Center for a New American Dream is an organization whose goal is to help Americans consume responsibly and thus protect the earth's resources and improve the quality of life. The center publishes booklets and newsletters, including the monthly publication *Take Action*.

Competitive Enterprise Institute (CEI)
1899 L Street NW, 12th Floor, Washington, DC   20036
(202) 331-1010 • fax: (202) 331-0640
e-mail: info@cei.org
Web site: www.cei.org

Competitive Enterprise Institute (CEI) is a nonprofit public policy organization dedicated to advancing the principles of free enterprise and limited government. It believes that individuals are best helped not by government intervention, but by making their own choices in a free marketplace. CEI's publications include the *CEI Weekly* newsletter and the bimonthly newsletter *CEI Planet.*

Economic Policy Institute (EPI)
1333 H Street NW, Suite 300, East Tower
Washington, DC   20005-4707
(202) 775-8810 • fax: (202) 775-0819
e-mail: researchdept@epi.org
Web site: www.epi.org

The Economic Policy Institute (EPI) is a nonprofit, nonpartisan think tank that seeks to broaden the public debate about strategies to achieve a prosperous and fair economy. The EPI Web site includes current information on U.S. gross domestic product, family income, international trade, jobs, and wages, and features publications including the weekly newsletter *EPI News.*

Federal Trade Commission (FTC)
600 Pennsylvania Avenue NW, Washington, DC   20580
(877) FTC-HELP (382-4357)
Web site: www.ftc.gov

The Federal Trade Commission (FTC) works to ensure that the nation's markets are vigorous, efficient, and free of restrictions that harm consumers. The FTC enforces federal consumer protection laws that prevent fraud, deception, and unfair business practices; the organization also combats identity theft, Internet scams, and telemarketing fraud. Publications posted on the FTC Web site include articles, research, and reports on economic issues.

Heritage Foundation
214 Massachusetts Avenue NE, Washington, DC   20002-4999
(202) 546-4400 • fax: (202) 544-2260
e-mail: info@heritage.org
Web site: www.heritage.org

The Heritage Foundation is a conservative public policy research institute that supports the principles of free enterprise and limited government in environmental matters. Its many publications include the daily e-newsletter the *Morning Bell* and economics-related articles such as "How to Protect Consumers in the Financial Marketplace: An Alternate Approach" and "Senator Dodd's Regulation Plan: 14 Fatal Flaws."

Hoover Institution
434 Galvez Mall, Stanford University
Stanford, CA   94305-6010
(650) 723-1754 • fax: (650) 723-1687
Web site: www.hoover.org

Founded in 1919 by future president Herbert Hoover, the Hoover Institution is a public policy research center devoted to advanced study of politics, economics, and political economy—both domestic and foreign—as well as international affairs. It publishes the quarterly *Hoover Digest* as well as a newsletter and special reports.

Hudson Institute
1015 Fifteenth Street NW, 6th Floor, Washington, DC   20005
(202) 974-2400 • fax: (202) 974-2410
e-mail: info@hudson.org
Web site: www.hudson.org

The Hudson Institute is a nonpartisan policy research organization that aims to challenge conventional thinking and help manage strategic transitions to the future through interdisciplinary and collaborative studies in defense, international relations, economics, culture, science, technology, and law.

Progressive Policy Institute (PPI)
1730 Rhode Island Avenue NW, Suite 308
Washington, DC   20036
(202) 525-3926 • fax: (202) 525-3941
Web site: www.ppionline.org

Progressive Policy Institute (PPI) is a public policy research organization that strives to develop alternatives to the traditional debate between liberals and conservatives. It advocates economic policies designed to stimulate broad upward mobility and social policies designed to liberate the poor from poverty and dependence. The institute publishes the book *Building the Bridge: 10 Big Ideas to Transform America*.

RAND Corporation
1776 Main Street, PO Box 2138
Santa Monica, CA   90407-2138
(310) 393-0411 X 7534 • fax: (310) 393-4818
Web site: www.rand.org

The RAND Corporation is a nonprofit research organization that performs policy analysis on critical social and economic issues such as education, poverty, crime, and the environment, as well as a range of national security issues.

Reason Foundation
3415 South Sepulveda Boulevard, Suite 400
Los Angeles, CA   90034
(310) 391-2245 • fax: (310) 391-4395
Web site: www.reason.org

The Reason Foundation works to provide a better understanding of the intellectual basis of a free society and to develop new ideas in public policy making. It researches contemporary social, economic, urban, and political problems. It publishes the newsletter *Privatization Watch* and the monthly *Reason* magazine.

Bibliography

Books

Yuval Elmelech   *Transmitting Inequality: Wealth and the American Family.* Lanham, MD: Rowman & Littlefield, 2008.

Joel L. Fleishman   *The Foundation: A Great American Secret: How Private Wealth Is Changing the World.* New York: PublicAffairs, 2007.

Robert Frank   *Richistan: A Journey Through the American Wealth Boom and the Lives of the New Rich.* New York: Three Rivers Press, 2007.

Norton Garfinkle   *The American Dream vs. the Gospel of Wealth: The Fight for a Productive Middle-Class Economy.* New Haven, CT: Yale University Press, 2006.

John Steele Gordon *An Empire of Wealth: The Epic History of American Economic Power.* New York: HarperCollins, 2004.

Heather Beth Johnson *The American Dream and the Power of Wealth: Choosing Schools and Inheriting Inequality in the Land of Opportunity.* New York: Routledge, 2006.

Ralph Nader   *"Only the Super-Rich Can Save Us!"* New York: Seven Stories Press, 2009.

Kevin Phillips

The Politics of Rich and Poor: Wealth and the American Electorate in the Reagan Aftermath. New York: Random House, 1990.

Kevin Phillips

Wealth and Democracy: A Political History of the American Rich. New York: Broadway Books, 2002.

Russ Alan Prince

The Middle-Class Millionaire: The Rise of the New Rich and How They Are Changing America. New York: Currency/Doubleday, 2008.

Jim Rubens

OverSuccess: Healing the American Obsession with Wealth, Fame, Power, and Perfection. Austin, TX: Greenleaf Book Group, 2008.

Larry Samuel

Rich: The Rise and Fall of American Wealth Culture. New York: AMACOM/American Management Association, 2009.

Keith Cameron Smith

The Top 10 Distinctions Between Millionaires and the Middle Class. New York: Ballantine Books, 2007.

Jim Taylor, Doug Harrison, and Stephen Kraus

The New Elite: Inside the Minds of the Truly Wealthy. New York: AMACOM/American Management Association, 2009.

Periodicals

Dean Baker

"Tax the Rich!" *Synthesis/ Regeneration*, Fall 2009.

William Baldwin — "When Capital Finds No Place to Hide," *Forbes*, March 30, 2009.

Ying Chu — "The New Trophy Wives: Asian Women," *Marie Claire*, September 2009.

Charles Crumpley — "A Wealth of Movement," *Los Angeles Business Journal*, May 22, 2009.

Daniel Fisher, Steven Bertoni, and Devon Pendleton — "Keeping Your Toys," *Forbes*, May 11, 2009.

Daniel Fisher, Steven Bertoni, and Devon Pendleton — "Survivor's Guide for the Affluent," *Forbes*, May 11, 2009.

David A. Kaplan — "The Yachting Class Sails Along," *Fortune*, April 4, 2009.

Gene J. Koprowski — "Judis: Taxing the Rich Makes Sense," *Newsmax*, July 21, 2009.

Gene J. Koprowski — "Obama Adviser: Rich People Killed Economy," *Newsmax*, March 17, 2009.

Luisa Kroll, Matthew Miller, and Tatiana Serafin, eds. — "Billionaire Bust: Who's Survived the Crash? Who's Getting Clobbered?" *Forbes*, March 30, 2009.

Raymond J. Lawrence — "A Country Awash in Money but Going Broke," *CounterPunch*, February 6–8, 2009.

Gerri Leder   "The Newly Rich Psyche," *On Wall Street*, January 2008.

Tom Prugh   "Less Stuff, or More Blood," *World Watch*, September–October 2009.

Robert J. Samuelson   "How the Mighty Have Fallen," *Newsweek*, July 11, 2009.

Peter Singer   "The Science Behind Our Generosity," *Newsweek*, February 28, 2009.

Aliya Sternstein   "Wealthy, Well-Educated More Likely to Engage in Online Civic Activities," NextGov.com, September 1, 2009.

Andrew Stuttaford   "Millionaires' Brawl," *Weekly Standard*, June 8, 2009.

Robert Tyndall   "Waiting for Wall Street," *Research*, August 1, 2009.

Dan Weil   "Billionaire Philanthropists Met Secretly in NYC," *Newsmax*, May 20, 2009.

Index